NLP

neuro
linguistic
programming

the new
art and
science of
getting
what
you want

DR HARRY ALDER

To Joy, Debbie
and Marcus

© 1994 Dr Harry Alder

First published in 1994 by
Piatkus Books Limited
5 Windmill Street, London W1P 1HF
e-mail: info@piatkus.co.uk

First paperback edition 1995

Reprinted 1995, 2001, 2002, 2004

*A catalogue record for this book
is available from the British Library*

ISBN 0–7499–1430–0 (Hbk)
ISBN 0–7499–1489–0 (Pbk)

Edited by Kelly Davis
Designed by Chris Warner

Typeset by Professional Data Bureau, London SW17
Printed and bound in Great Britain by Biddles Ltd, King's Lynn, Norfolk

NLP

Other books by Harry Alder

THE RIGHT BRAIN MANAGER (Piatkus)
NLP IN 21 DAYS with Beryl Heather (Piatkus)

Contents

▼

Introduction

▼

NEURO-LINGUISTIC PROGRAMMING is concerned with how top people in different fields obtain outstanding results, and how their successful thinking and behaviour patterns can be copied. It is concerned with what happens when we *think*, and the effect of our thinking on our behaviour, and the behaviour of others. It shows us how we can think better, and thus achieve more. NLP teaches us how to communicate, inwardly and outwardly, in a way that can make the difference between mediocrity and excellence. But, rather than simply adding more to the theory of communication, NLP is very practical. It models the way outstanding performers think and act, in a way that you and I can use to bring about similar outstanding results. Most of the techniques I describe in this book can be tried out straight away so you can enjoy getting results in different areas of your life while learning, then build on your successes.

NLP is also very adaptable. If a particular technique doesn't work immediately, it allows you to change what you do and the way you think about your specific circumstance or problem until you get what you are after. Once you have grasped a few fundamental principles, you can make these changes easily, thereby gaining a better understanding of the way you, as an individual, think and the way your thought processes affect your behaviour — and consequently your achievements. NLP provides a whole range of mental techniques for change that enable you to take control of your life.

NLP is both an art and a science of personal excellence. It is an art, because the way we think and act is unique to each of us, and any description — especially of feelings, attitudes and beliefs — is bound to be highly subjective. It is also a science, although still embryonic, because it incorporates well-researched methods that can be used to identify the patterns of successful behaviour.

It all started in the early 1970s when John Grinder, a linguist, and Richard Bandler, a mathematician, psychotherapist and computer expert, studied the methods of three leading psychotherapists, who were consistently able to bring about outstanding changes in human behaviour. Dr Milton H. Erickson has been described as one of the greatest hypnotherapists of all time, while Virginia Satir is an outstanding family therapist who has been able to bring about seemingly insurmountable resolution of relationship problems. Gregory Bateson, a British anthroplogist, as well as providing a model of outstanding performance, greatly influenced the founders of NLP, Grinder and Bandler, in their early work. The methods they developed have since been applied in the fields of sport, business, government and personal development, attracting a large and growing worldwide following.

The impact of NLP has already been far-reaching, as its applications have spread to more and more areas of human life. Its simple but profound concepts and track record of practical success have resulted in its remarkable growth, and it now challenges the position of orthodox psychology in its relevance to ordinary people. At the same time it renders generations of self-development and positive thinking books very incomplete and dated.

Although the subject is relatively new, there is no shortage of literature. However, many of the books only cover specific aspects of NLP and can be intimidating to the novice. Many of these were written by authors with backgrounds in psychotherapy or hypnotherapy and the style of the literature reflects this. Not surprisingly, jargon has evolved, partly reflecting the specialised backgrounds of the originators (a linguist and a psychologist) and partly to express some of the new and specialised concepts that any science accumulates. Even in everyday conversation a so-called NLP practitioner might refer to an effective technique as 'elegant' or the rapport between individuals as a 'dance'.

Little has been written for businesspeople or the man in the street, the choice being largely limited to either shallow, popularised versions of the subject, or full-blown text books. This book will, I hope, fill the gap. It includes the main principles and a number of proven techniques you can use immediately. It would not have been possible to cover the whole subject in a volume of this size, so I have had to be selective. In this selection process I have taken an attitude of healthy scepticism and excluded anything that seemed 'hard to swallow' or 'a bit heavy'. I have omitted, for example, any reference to hypnotherapy, because of its mystical connotations in the minds of some readers. Techniques to cure major phobias in half an hour or so (that have already benefited, as it happens, thousands of people) also failed this 'credibility test', although I do describe plenty of techniques for changing all sorts of long-standing habits and achieving more or less any personal goal. Similarly, some NLP methods are more appropriate for a therapy situation and are excluded because they do not fit my DIY requirement. But if you are new or fairly new to NLP, I hope you will find here as much as you can usefully use in a few months, and certainly enough to bring about fundamental improvements in goal-achievement, personal confidence and lifestyle. For those who want to know more, I suggest further reading at the end of the book.

Why the name? The *Neuro* part of NLP refers to the neurological processes of seeing, hearing, feeling, tasting and smelling — the senses that we use for inner thought processes as well as for experiencing the outside world. All our understanding, and what we describe as consciousness, comes through these neural windows to our brain. *Linguistic* recognises the part that language plays, both in our communication with others, and also in how we organise our thoughts. NLP helps us to use everyday language for better thinking and more successful behaviour. *Programming* refers to the way we can program our own thoughts and behaviour, much as a computer is programmed to do specific things.

In summary, NLP deals with the way we filter, through our five senses, our experiences of the outside world, and how we use those same inner senses, both intentionally and unintentionally, to achieve the results we desire. It is all about how we perceive or think. And it is our thinking — perception, imagination, patterns of belief — that determines what we do, and what we achieve. The subject is evolving rapidly, as new discoveries are continually being made about the workings of the brain, so any explanation is sure to be incomplete. But for the time being NLP can be defined as 'the art and science of personal excellence'.

1

Getting What You Want

▼

CHRISTY BROWN, the Irish novelist, could only move his left foot. Born with cerebral palsy, unable to speak, walk or feed himself, he later taught himself to read, paint and type. Against all the odds he became a major literary figure and succeeded in getting what he wanted. He described the freedom his efforts brought:

> I wrote and wrote without pause, without consciousness of my surroundings, hour after hour. I felt a different person. I wasn't unhappy any more. I didn't feel frustrated or shut up any more. I was free, I could think, I could live, I could create. . . .I felt released, at peace, I could be myself. . . . And if I couldn't know the joy of dancing I could know the ecstasy of creating.

The desire for human excellence is relentless. When we see excellence in others — whether we envy, admire or even idolise them — it has a unique attraction. We tend to be drawn to examples of the best in human achievement. And whenever we see such displays we see a little bit of ourselves; a higher or deeper part of us that seems to know there is something more, something better to strive for. Whatever we want to have, or do, or be, the desire for excellence seems to be universal. The mystery is why some, like Christy Brown with everything against him, find what they are looking for, while so many others fall short of their dreams.

Success has been equated for a long time in Western culture with material possessions, the trappings of status and power. Yet our newspapers and television channels are full of stories of entertainers, sportspeople or statesmen who have every conceivable luxury and can command any sort of lifestyle but still feel like failures. Many have even shortened their lives through the excesses of their so-called 'success'. Most of us know a friend or colleague who, in terms of material wealth, or even the good health that we all rate so highly, can hardly be described as successful according to society's usual criteria. Yet they have a degree of contentment, fulfilment and genuine happiness that we envy. Somehow, they have got what they want; they are doing what they want to do.

Models of true success are resourceful learners, able to transcend their own thoughts and see the big picture, ready to discard outmoded ways of thinking in favour of more appropriate ones that get them what they want. They use challenges; they use failures; they use random, seemingly negative, circumstances and events to bring about mastery, creativity and success. That is what this book is all about — how you can get what you want, do what you want to do, and be what you want to be. In the 1950s and 1960s a vast array of 'positive thinking' and other self development books appeared. These were mostly read by positive thinkers, who amassed more and more volumes as new claims were made and new systems or philosophies were revealed. Their instinctive optimistic attitude was fuelled in a self-fulfilling way by each new book or concept. A smaller category of readers invested less enthusiastically in the far-fetched but tempting panaceas offered. In these cases, any early improvement in thinking was short-lived. They soon fell back into more comfortable, familiar, negative attitudes and beliefs, the odd failure neatly labelled 'typical' and the odd success a 'fluke'. Any close examination of the evangelistic positive thinking of that period reveals, however, more rhetoric than substance, and a research base that was anecdotal rather than scientific.

There have been changes. Along with amazing developments in the worlds of computers, communications and cosmology, there have been important though less widely-understood advances. The work of Roger Sperry in the 1960s, Nobel prize winner in physiology, gave us remarkable new insights into the way the human brain works. Some cherished ideas have been overtaken for good. For example, the finding that the two sides of the brain (specifically the upper part, or cerebral cortex) operate effectively as two minds has changed the way we now understand human thought and behaviour. Likewise, evidence that a lifetime of detailed experience is stored on the 'hard disk' of the brain, and is accessible, has changed our understanding of intuition, memory and the whole process of thought. And having learned that the number of potential neural connections in a single human brain is *greater that the estimated total number of atoms in the known universe*, we have begun to ask whether there is more we can do with this 'lump of grey matter'. In short, the human brain seems to offer godlike understanding of ourselves, our fellow beings and our environment, as well as vast, untapped potential for achievement — for getting what we want.

The science of Neuro-Linguistic Programming, or NLP as it is popularly known, has consolidated a lot of these advances and given us, for the first time, a structure for the study of excellence in human behaviour and communication. In other words, we now have a scientific approach to the highly subjective but universally interesting subject of getting what we want. Having said this, NLP does not compare, even remotely, with the physical sciences — human beings have never been ideal laboratory subjects, and their behaviour patterns, let alone thinking processes, defy .the orthodox rules of scientific method. The human brain seems to occupy a special place in the overall scheme of things. But NLP does provide a basis for describing and communicating thought processes, the building blocks of feelings, attitudes and beliefs which in turn create behaviour. It offers a structured approach to the part language plays in thinking and interpersonal communication. And, uniquely, it provides a framework for copying, or modelling, human excellence. Skills, abilities and even so-called thinking strategies can be transferred from one person to another. Most importantly, and this is where NLP differs from almost all branches of psychology and other therapies involving personal behaviour, it produces remarkable results in a very short space of time. And most of the principles and techniques can be applied without calling on therapists, consultants or gurus. It is largely DIY.

My aim in this book is not to produce a layman's guide to NLP, but rather a layman's guide to getting what you want. It so happens that NLP provides the proven techniques that bring habitual goal achievement within reach of every one of us. The subject is no longer hit or miss. It is no longer hype and rhetoric. It no longer needs to be, as evidence mounts and sceptical, pragmatic people from all walks of life begin to see the benefits for themselves.

SUCCESS FACTORS

As human beings we all have an inner goal-achieving instinct. This might not rise to changing society or making a historical impact; it might be confined to your family life, your garden or a single, consuming hobby or interest. But we all have purposes that drive us, even though we cannot always articulate or even recognise them. More than this, wherever we see people succeeding, the same factors seem to appear time and time again. These factors do not give us a ready-made formula — people are so different in their personalities, talents and resources — but they do give us clues as to the essential elements.

 We always find, for instance, a drive, enthusiasm or passion — call it what you will — which seems to be linked with a clarity of purpose, or vision. Some dream or goal gets a person enthused. We find strong beliefs — not necessarily of a religious sort, but beliefs about yourself, what you are capable of doing, and the people you relate to. And, linked with these, there is usually a strong system of values, whatever those values are. (Core values are surprisingly universal across cultures and religions, and have been over the centuries.) We also notice that successful people, as well as knowing where they want to be, usually seem to follow some plan or strategy.

They seem organised in their thinking and the way they marshal internal and external resources. This applies to successful sportspeople, businesspeople, parents, artists, musicians and people in other creative professions. They also seem to have a certain energy — not just physical strength and fitness, but an inner energy that keeps them going against all the odds when ordinary people would have given up. Like their beliefs, values and vision, few would attribute this special energy to genetic, educational or cultural background. It just seems to be part and parcel of the striving after a goal, or dream, that we all, as purposeful beings, understand. Finally, they have the ability to *communicate*, at whatever level and in whatever way is needed to bring about their success.

You do not need a special science to identify these characteristics in successful people. What NLP offers is the ability to understand how these traits, and others, work in specific individuals. It then shows us how to copy or model their successful thinking strategies and behaviour, without the years of trial and error. Once the process, rather than the content, of successful behaviour is known, such excellence is within everyone's reach.

FOUR STEPS TO SUCCESS

There are four essential steps to getting what you want. They are simple, but awesomely profound. They are the basis of all human success, and the foundation of NLP. If you are committed to achieving your desires, these steps are sufficient, even without further support or explanation, to make significant changes in your life for the better. When reinforced with the specific principles and techniques described in this book, they provide all the technology you need to get what you want.

1.   *Know what you want*

NLP talks about knowing your *outcome* — the result you want to achieve. Any successful person knows what he or she wants. This is what marks out achievers. If you are not particularly ambitious, or goal-oriented, it might not seem natural to state your goals in a specific way. But you can start somewhere. We all have wishes and dreams, including those that will ultimately benefit family and friends, or the wider community. There may be habits you want to change, or skills and abilities you admire in others that you would like to have yourself. All these can be expressed as what NLP calls *outcomes*, enabling you to *become* a goal-achieving person. And this is as good a time as any to start. In the next chapter you will learn some simple rules to ensure that your goals are stated clearly. Having clearly expressed outcomes gives you the maximum chance of fulfilling them.

2.   *Take action*

Do what you think will bring about the achievement of your desire. This sounds very obvious, but the main characteristic of high achievers is that they actually start to do the things that others just talk and dream about. What you do might not always work, so there is an element of personal risk. But you will never know until you act.

3. Learn to notice the results of what you do

This requires what is called 'sensory acuity'. You need to be able to observe accurately the things that happen as a result of your behaviour — whether your actions are bringing you nearer to achieving your outcome. You also need to spot the signals, or negative feedback, that show when you are off course. A lot of NLP is to do with understanding how we sense things, interpret them, and feed the information back into further actions.

4. Be prepared to change your behaviour until you get the result you are after

Based on sensory feedback, you must always be ready to do something else. If at first you don't succeed, try something different! Sometimes this requires creative thinking on your part, and this book suggests plenty of ways to generate ideas for new approaches and different behaviour.

These four steps are so simple that there is a danger of ignoring them and looking for something more complex and demanding. Another common mistake is to miss out one stage — such as being willing to *do* something, even when you are not sure exactly what result it will bring, or being willing to *change your behaviour*, when you would prefer to stay with a more predictable, risk-free way of behaving. But if you spend time observing people who have done worthwhile things with their lives, including people you know well, you will begin to see this pattern of important steps in every success they achieve. These simple steps are sometimes demanding, at least initially, but there is always a price to pay for getting anything worthwhile. Rest assured that your investment will be repaid many times over and, as with other demanding activities, there can be almost as much pleasure in the journey as in reaching the destination.

NLP PRESUPPOSITIONS

Like any branch of science, NLP is based on a number of principles. However, these principles are far more flexible than the laws that apply to the physical sciences. They should be regarded not so much as true, but useful. (For example, the statement that it always rains in the Lake District may not be true, but it may be useful.) I will describe some of these principles at the outset in order to give you a flavour of the subject as a whole. They will also form a foundation for some of the techniques you will learn later. An understanding of these principles alone — or presuppositions as they are sometimes called — can bring about remarkable improvements in performance when they are applied to everyday situations. Here are some of the major principles.

The map is not the territory

We each interpret what is going on around us through our five senses. What you believe about what you see, hear and feel is based on your own lifetime of experience which filters any information coming to you through your senses. What seems good to you might seem bad to me. What is useful to me might be of no use to you. Our unique interpretation of everything around us builds up into a personal mental map. This personal map is our reality — our understanding or consciousness. But your map is different to mine. We each see things differently. And none of our maps is objective reality. That is, they are not the *territory* of the outside, objective world; they are only subjective interpretations. That we can never know the territory itself is both frustrating and humbling. Instead we have to make do with our unique, personal maps which remain subjective, however hard we try to record accurately what we see, hear and feel. You may be convinced that a terrorist is not a freedom fighter, that heroism is not foolhardiness, that Mary is confident rather than pushy. But my map might interpret the same objective reality very differently. Neither of us can claim to perceive objectively; we have simply filtered the facts and circumstances differently. We all hold different beliefs about a multitude of everyday things. We have different maps of the same territory.

Although this metaphor may seem simple, it has profound implications. It certainly accounts for all the wars and untold misery caused by differing maps of the same territory. At the same time it opens up the possibility of understanding other people's perceptions and the enormous benefits of better communication.

Understanding how someone's map differs from yours not only avoids all the wasted time and effort of bad communication, but also lets you know what makes other people tick and how you can influence them to help you reach your goals.

Although our behaviour might seem inappropriate, or even bizarre or irrational, to others, it always 'makes sense' in the context of our own mental map. We do what is best within our unique and very limited view of reality.

Underlying all behaviour is a positive intention

NLP makes a distinction between our behaviour and our intentions: what we do and what we want to achieve. There is a positive intention behind everything we do. We are always aiming towards some goal which is positive and worthwhile to us, whatever others may think. Even an action like smoking is likely to have some underlying positive intention — perhaps the desire to be more relaxed, or to be accepted in a particular social setting.

To take another example, a man who spends very little time with his family might well think he is acting in their best interests, by trying hard to earn a living, furthering his career and seeking to secure their future. However misguided his behaviour may seem to others, his intention is positive. Sometimes our intentions are not clear at a conscious level and may, as in the case of smoking, be complex and conflicting. But a little reflection will usually identify the intention behind the behaviour. By understanding this principle you can get rid of unwanted behaviours, not by 'trying' and applying will power, but by recognising the positive intention and finding other ways to achieve it. There is usually another way, a better way, of satisfying the same intention.

Choice is better than no choice

Having choices means having greater freedom to act, and also having a greater chance of achieving what you want. Much of NLP is concerned with opening up more choices or ideas. We are often surprised at how many

15

ingenious ideas we can come up with when we are in a creative state of mind. These creative times can occur at any time — when you are in the shower, driving, or even when you wake in the middle of the night. They provide insights into problems and give us choices.

NLP puts it in this way: one option is no option; two options may be a dilemma; three or more options give you the freedom to best achieve your goals. If you doubt your ability to come up with options, this book contains a variety of techniques, involving the way you use language, and how you 'see' situations, that will enable you to tap the limitless creativity of your brain.

The meaning of your communication is the response it produces

If a communication does not produce the desired effect, our usual instinct is to blame the person on the receiving end. 'She just wouldn't listen.' 'It's there in black and white.' Reverting to the earlier metaphor, we assume that our own map is the same as the other person's — and the message, although communicated as simply and unambiguously as possible, reflects this fallacy. In addition to the basic message, our tone of voice and body language also betray our feelings, attitudes and beliefs (our personal map) and all this is part of any communication. No wonder there is so much scope for misunderstanding and communication breakdown.

An alternative approach to communication is to treat the result (whatever it is) simply as information. Then we can change our behaviour, repeatedly if need be, until the desired effect is obtained. This takes the emotion out of the situation or relationship, and concentrates our minds on what the communication is all about — achieving a particular outcome or effect. Although this trial and error method can take time, and puts a heavy onus of responsibility on the communicator, at least the effort is not wasted. We eventually succeed in our intention. The process of communicating is just a means to that end, and can be changed or terminated as required. But the extra thought we put into the way we communicate is an investment, because what we learn through 'negative feedback' is bound to be of value in the future. So be willing to change. If you always do what you've always done, you'll always get what you've always got!

We gradually learn to get our message across, and the things to do and say that best bring about the results we want. Soon we become excellent communicators and we learn to be effective in achieving the goals we set ourselves. This perspective on communication gives us power and extra choice so that we are not at the mercy of other people's differing perceptions and beliefs. With power, however, comes the responsibility for our own actions, for achieving the things we want to achieve. And remember, it is easier to change yourself than others. So this is the measure of effective communication: not the words used or the medium or the technological aids, but whether the desired results are achieved.

There is no failure, only feedback

If things do not work out the way we plan, we usually think we have failed. But the NLP view is that what happens is neither good nor bad, but merely information. If you crunched the gears when learning to drive, it did not mean that you failed as a driver — just that you learned the results of changing gear in that particular way, changed your behaviour, and benefited accordingly. You used information, or feedback, to improve. This is an important distinction, as a sense of failure (an aspect of our personal map rather than reality), and the lower self-image it creates, will always affect our behaviour adversely. Failure, or a lower level of achievement, becomes a self-fulfilling subconscious goal. When the very concept of failure is eliminated from your map, all kinds of new possibilities open up. You keep going when others give up. Do you recognise the following potted biography?

> Failed in business at age 31.
> Was defeated in a legislative race at age 32.
> Failed again in business at age 34.
> Experienced the death of his sweetheart at age 35.
> Had a nervous breakdown at age 36.
> Lost an election at age 38.
> Lost a congressional race at age 43.
> Lost a congressional race at age 46.
> Lost a congressional race at age 48.
> Lost a senatorial race at age 55.
> Failed in an effort to become vice-president of the USA at age 56.
> Lost a senatorial race at age 58.
> Was elected president at the age of 60.

The man's name was Abraham Lincoln. And he was not the only historical figure to experience many 'failures' on his way to achievement. Thomas Edison, after trying 9,999 ways to perfect the electric light bulb, insisted: 'I didn't fail. I just discovered another way not to invent the electric light bulb.' In fact the list of successful people who have demonstrated this principle is endless. It also illustrates the four steps to success we discussed earlier. The *attitude* that it produces is what keeps you going, and makes you stand out from the crowd. You learn from every so-called mistake, and thus turn every outcome — however negative or painful at the time — to your advantage. You start to recognise the behaviour that gets results, and adjust your priorities in time and effort accordingly.

A BETTER WAY TO LEARN

You will gather from these principles that NLP is concerned with learning from what we observe, and basing our actions on what we learn. So these presuppositions are as much to do with learning — in the widest sense — as with communication and goal-achievement. But we need to learn in the adventurous, enjoyable, exciting way that a young child learns, rather than the way we have come to expect from teachers in school or college. This ability to learn as you go, and learn effectively, usually without a teacher, is one of the most important benefits you will receive from NLP.

People who reach personal excellence in any particular sphere are often unaware of their excellence until it is pointed out. Moreover, they often cannot explain what they do or how they do it. Their skill has reached a level at which they operate unconsciously. A champion tennis player, in the closing moments of the match, might be consciously thinking about where he wants the ball to land, or the cup he is soon to receive, or a hot shower and a comfortable bed; he will not be thinking of the nuances of his forehand or the footwork which he does automatically. He is unconscious of the magical skills that keep his spectators spellbound. Indeed, as Timothy Gallwey explains in his book *The Inner Game of Tennis*, by thinking about such skills, he would, in fact, become less competent, lose his 'flow', and probably ruin his chances of success. This also applies to you and me the moment we start to think about exactly how we drive a car — the clutch movements, our hands on the steering wheel, and a dozen other automatic skills we have perfected to a level of 'unconscious competence'.

So if this level of unconscious mastery is the ultimate aim in any skill or activity, where do we start? Initially we are all in a state of what might be called unconscious ignorance (as regards knowledge) or unconscious incompetence (as regards a skill or ability). In other words, we don't know what we don't know, or what we might be able to do. According to the first NLP principle, the knowledge or skill is outside our present mental map of the world. I'm sure that now and again you stumble across some subject or situation that you did not even know existed. From that moment you leave your state of blissful unconscious ignorance or incompetence, and enter a state of conscious incompetence. You now know that you don't know or cannot do something.

When trying to learn any new bit of knowledge or acquire a new skill — from baking a souffle or changing a car tyre to speaking a foreign language — we operate in this learning mode of being incompetent but knowing it. Having acquired competence and knowledge, we then move into a learning stage of conscious competence. You know you can do something, and are good at it, at least to some degree. We all aspire to include more and more activities in this category, from sporting or academic achievement to professional competence or personal relationships.

The last stage in this learning ladder is by far the most important from an NLP point of view. At a given level of expertise we are simply not aware of our competence. We can do things without knowing exactly how we are doing them, and we do not need to think about them consciously. Even world experts often cannot explain how they accomplish what they do — to them it just comes naturally. They do not really try.

We can only think of one thing at a time at a highly conscious level, although we can juggle up to perhaps five or six. So for any complex activity, from driving a car to eating spare ribs (while sitting on a chair, holding a conversation, watching a two-year-old, and listening for the start of the TV news), we need to call on our 'autopilot'. This is what enables us to do routine things, like shaving, getting dressed, or cleaning the windows, without thinking about them. When we are on autopilot, which is most of the time, we are not conscious of everything that is happening, just one or two activities that require high level, conscious attention (such as a specific point we are making in conversation, or a headache coming on). Eating the spare ribs, or showering, or filling the washing machine has become an activity in the unconscious competence category.

Based on this learning ladder, and some NLP goal-achieving techniques, you can relegate (or elevate, however you see it) just about any skill to a level of unconscious competence. There is no limit to what the human brain can learn to accomplish in such a way. Having reached this level of learning, people run businesses, carry out amazing feats of memory, hold an audience captive with their musical virtuosity, or write 50 books in a single year. To them it is no big deal — they do not think about it. This kind of learning uses the whole brain, the conscious left side and the unconscious right side, applying thinking strategies that work. The aim with any NLP skill is to use it in an intuitive way. As with learning any worthwhile physical skill, it takes some conscious effort and practice at first.

unconscious competence

↑

conscious competence

↑

conscious incompetence

↑

unconscious incompetence

Sometimes we have to *unlearn* something — like correcting a tennis swing or getting out of bad habits when driving a car. This involves going back from unconscious competence (when we act without thinking) to conscious incompetence. *Relearning* involves moving from conscious incompetence, back through conscious competence to unconscious competence — having opened up more choices and gained a higher level of mastery.

These are some of the fundamental principles of NLP as they affect our thinking, behaviour and learning. We shall meet others. And I shall describe techniques that allow you to get the most from these simple but far-reaching presuppositions.

But everything depends on you. In the following chapters you will learn proven techniques to apply these principles to any area of your life. They have been drawn from observation of thousands of highly successful people in their various fields and form a technology that always produces results when followed with commitment. But only you can make the decision to change, to start on the road to achieving what you are truly capable of. It is time to raise your standards, change limiting beliefs, and adopt strategies that give you results. It is time to make decisions.

TIME TO DECIDE

What is important to you right now will dictate the direction of your life. What you *decide* now will create your very future. You are what you are today because of decisions that you made, or did not make, some time in the past. And your decisions will determine where you will be ten years from now. Human excellence is about taking control of your life. We gain that control by our actions. And our actions are determined by the decisions we make.

Deciding means committing. There is a world of difference between merely having an interest in something ('I think I'd like to have that, or do so-and so') and committing yourself to a certain goal ('I'm going to do that'). Most people make excuses for not having achieved the many things they would have liked to. What will separate you from so many others is not your knowledge of what to do and how to do it, but your commitment to change and action. If you want to give up smoking, you have to make an irreversible decision. If you want to learn a language, you have to translate interest into commitment — you have to decide. We are all able to make decisions — it is an inbuilt faculty — but many of us are a little rusty. We need to make more of them, on a daily basis, as every decision, however small, triggers the actions that eventually get results. It is well worth getting into practice because, once you really decide to do something, you can do almost anything you want. Start by deciding to follow seriously the techniques you will learn in this book. Decide to gain the information and skills to put the 21 Day Action Plan into practice. Decide to evaluate suggestions simply on the basis of whether or not they work.

In the next chapter you will be deciding on your goals. Some of these may be very short term, while others reflect your beliefs and values and will affect your whole life. So, as well as deciding what to *do*, you will be deciding what is important to you and what is not; what to concentrate on, and what to put in second place. At every level, you have to decide.

This frightens many people. And the fear is usually about making the wrong decision. So the first decision to make is not to be afraid of failure, to be willing to give things a try, even though success is never 100 per cent guaranteed. The only guarantee is that if you don't do anything, you'll never get anything. Achievers are always willing to 'fail'; every one of them does so (some repeatedly) but they seldom use the word 'fail'. They know they have to start by doing something, that they have to be willing to change as they go along, and that they have to keep going for their goal against all the odds. So don't be afraid of making wrong decisions. You will be in the company of some of the world's very best. Decide now to take your first step towards getting what you want, by learning how to set clear goals.

2

Setting Your Goals

▼

THE FIRST STEP TO SUCCESS is knowing what you want — what you want to have, what you want to be, or what you want to achieve. NLP does not create your goals and desires — only *you* can decide what you really want — but it helps you clarify any desires you have, and offers you ways of fulfilling them.

It has long been known that 'achievers' tend to be goal-oriented. In a study carried out at Yale University in 1953 students were asked if they had specific, written-down goals and a plan for achieving them. Only 3 per cent had such written goals. Twenty years later, the researchers interviewed all the surviving members of the 1953 class. They discovered that the 3 per cent with specific goals were worth more in financial terms than all the other 97 per cent put together. Although this sort of measurement does not tell the whole story (and success should certainly not be measured just in financial terms), other more subjective measures, such as the level of joy and happiness the graduates felt, also showed the same 3 per cent scoring highly.

Some people have difficulty in setting their goals, or maybe just haven't thought about setting them. The fact that you are reading this book probably means you are not in this category, but at the same time your goals may be more like wishes — not very clear, not very serious, and constantly changing. You may not see yourself as either ambitious or goal-oriented. But this may just be a matter of how we use language differently.

All human beings are super goal-achieving mechanisms. Hundreds of our life 'goals' — such as maintaining our breathing, pulse rate, and temperature — are being achieved all the time without our even realising it. Fortunately for all of us, these goals are programmed into our systems. But just because a non-ambitious person — perhaps described as a 'stick-in-the-mud' — does not set conscious goals, it does not mean that he or she is not goal-oriented. It takes a lot of willpower and single-mindedness, for example, to maintain the status quo in a constantly changing world. Leading a so-called 'quiet life', at least in my experience, is an ambitious goal in a high-speed world.

It is easy to assume that goals have to be visible and material. But we can have goals concerning our family, health, hobbies, sports activities or leisure time that might be largely intangible, and measured in quality rather than quantity. If your desire is to get off the treadmill of a job, career, or particular way of life, this is perhaps an even greater challenge than climbing the ladder of material success — and a no less worthwhile goal.

GOAL-ACHIEVERS AND DREAMERS

People set and express their goals in different ways. Some are systematic and highly organised, writing everything down and perhaps dividing their goals into short-term, medium-term and long-term. They will no doubt have a similar logical way of solving problems and making decisions such as changing job or moving house. Others do not set goals in any conscious, organised way, yet are nonetheless goal-oriented — having a clear mental picture or feeling of what they want to achieve. They are drawn more by a vision or a dream, as might be the case with Olympic medallists or outstanding entrepreneurs, but also anyone who can easily imagine a goal before it has happened — whether it be a better job, a sporting achievement or a re-landscaped garden. This difference is to do with the way we think, and specifically which side of the brain we tend to use most. The left side is better at conscious detailed thinking using logical processes and language. The right side is happier dealing in images and feelings, seems to bypass logic, and tends to view things 'holistically'.

NLP is very much about harnessing both sides of the brain in order to form clear goals that will have the best chance of success. Using your whole brain gives you a unique and formidable resource, enabling you to mix your dreams with common sense and get in touch with what you really want.

MAKE A LIST

First of all, make out your list of wants, desires, goals, wishes, outcomes — however you choose to describe them. At this stage your list can include *all* your goals, including those in the categories 'I fancy . . .', 'I wouldn't mind . . .', 'It would be nice if . . . .' Most of these will be eliminated later, but even if only one or two are eventually attained the whole exercise will be worthwhile. The purpose of this list is to establish your true, motivating goals, which will have a high chance of success. If you wish, you can categorise them into definite goals and wishes; and into short-term, medium-term and long-term. In the last category will come any major life goals; in the first category things you would like to achieve by next weekend, or perhaps by the end of the month. To set your goals, ask the following questions.

Are your goals specific?

Be clear about what you want, by being as specific as you can. Ask yourself: ' What exactly do I want?' Goals need to be 'sensory based'; what will you see, hear, feel, taste and smell? Ask yourself also: 'What is the situation now, and what will have to be *different* if I am to achieve my goal?' Be specific. If you want to learn a language, for example, what standard are you setting yourself — a few holiday phrases, or a proper working knowledge, including the grammar? And by when — in three months, six months or a year? Through self-study, evening classes or whatever? It will help if you put your goals in writing, because the act of committing a goal to paper in itself requires you to think more precisely about what you want. You should also try to think your goal through in some depth. Is there some other less obvious desire that this goal is trying to fulfil? Sometimes we really want qualifications or other outward signs of achievement because of the recognition and respect they bring. Or maybe we want them in order to further our careers, and at the same time to give us power, or status, or financial independence. As you think honestly about all this, you may want to change specific goals so that they are more in keeping with your underlying desires. Or you may replace them with entirely different goals which are more likely to achieve your deeper wants. As well as weeding out unclear or suspect desires, this process will increase your self-awareness in general.

'I want to be happy', whilst a worthwhile desire, does not meet this criterion of being specific, and you might want to measure such a goal against some of the following questions as well. By asking: 'What would make me happy?' you will start to identify achievable goals that will help you attain happiness.

Get to know about your goals. Enjoy reading about what you are aiming for and doing some research. As well as clearly defining what you want, start to align yourself with your goals, see yourself as having achieved them, and live out what you want to be.

Are your goals within your personal control?

Check that each goal is reasonably within your personal control. In other words, success or failure will largely depend on you, and you will not be able to produce a long list of excuses later if things do not work out. For example, if you want your boss's job, your success is heavily dependent on another person — who may stick around longer than you thought. Such a goal would not reflect your own success, but circumstances and events for which you can take neither the credit nor the blame. If, however, you aim to be in a position at the same level as your present boss within one year, not restricting yourself to a single company, or even industry, then you will have infinitely more personal control over the fulfilment of your goal. So you need to be specific about what you really want, which in the last example is probably the status, salary and recognition of a higher level job, rather than a higher level job in your present company.

If you have plans involving a team activity, some personal control is still important. You might well have goals for your own performance within a team, say in a sport or business, but to have strong goals for the whole team would take the situation outside your personal scope — unless you are the coach or manager, in which case you are the prime mover who can accept both praise and blame.

The essence of success is not just achieving goals, but achieving the *right* goals — for you. If, for instance, your goal for your child's success (and left in these terms it would be neither specific nor reasonably within your control, however well-meaning and expert a parent you were), you might break it into several goals, such as providing financially for the child's education, arranging a worthwhile holiday experience, offering help when the child eventually wishes to start up in business — or whatever. These interim goals can be quite specific, and very much within your (rather than your child's) control. Clarifying each goal, and imagining it being fulfilled, is also very motivating. So ask the question: 'What part will I have in achieving this outcome?' Then change what has to be changed, formulating different goals that will satisfy your underlying desire. A goal like 'I want interesting people to be attracted to me' would be better stated as 'I want to make friends with interesting people'. To bring things right down to a practical level, and make yourself central, ask 'What will I, personally, be doing to achieve my goal?' and 'How can I get things started?'

As long as we structure our lives in such a way that our happiness depends on things or people outside our control we can expect to experience pain and disappointment. Adjusting your goals so that you are the prime player puts their fulfilment within your own power.

Have you got what it takes to fulfil your goals?

This question focuses on the resources you have that can be utilised in achieving your goal. These personal resources include your natural abilities, health and strength, available time, intelligence and physical build. Don't let this scare you. You just have to be realistic, without underestimating your potential. For instance, if you want to get into the top ten in, say, tennis or boxing, and you are now 45, you would no doubt scrub that goal on the basis that you don't have what it takes. However, in other sports, and a thousand other areas, age would not be an obstacle. We can all quote examples of people who have overcome great personal handicaps in order to achieve their desires. So do not be too hard on yourself. People don't usually lack resources, they lack control over those resources, and that is a problem we can do something about.

Whilst what we might call 'intelligence' might be critical for a particularly cerebral scientific research job, the lack of it certainly would not preclude you from being a top managing director in many industries. The additional resources you will need for such a goal can usually be acquired by training, experience and hard work. So this question is to do with *innate* resources, rather than those that can be acquired, such as money or knowledge. If necessary you can amend your goal to fit your resources. So, for example, it might be quite feasible for you to sing in a local or even national choir (given your natural singing voice), whilst not rising to the world stage as a virtuoso soloist. In a sport, once past your 'sell by date' you might switch your aspirations to coaching younger people, or administering or managing, thus keeping your interest and enjoyment alive. But bear in mind that most of us tend to *underestimate* our potential. Learn from people like Christy Brown and others you know of who have dug deep enough to *find* the inner resources they needed to achieve success.

How will you know when you have achieved your goals?

Besides being specific about your goals, you should be able to measure your success in some way. So it helps to add to any desired outcome some tangible element that you will definitely experience. For instance, if you learn a language through a recognised course, you will almost certainly receive a certificate to show your level of achievement, and so you will know exactly when success has been achieved. In other cases fulfilling your goal might involve actually banking a cheque, visiting some faraway city, taking part in some public ceremony, or handling the completion statement on the sale or purchase of a house. The more tangible evidence you can bring to mind, in effect enjoying your success before it has happened, the more real and quantifiable your goal will become.

Are your goals expressed positively?

This means thinking about what you do want rather than what you don't want. So it is preferable if your goals are not expressed negatively (e.g. 'I will not have my house repossessed' or 'I will not be made redundant' or 'I will not be missed from the team selection next season'). Our brain is obtuse in some respects. When instructed 'Don't miss the plane, or the cricket ball' it only seems to hear the 'miss'. Any goal can be switched into a positive mode, by asking 'What would I rather have?' or 'What do I really want?'

Are your goals at the right level?

Is your goal big enough, or too big in view of your resources? If it is too big, ask 'What is preventing me from achieving this?' Then you can turn the problem into smaller goals that are achievable. This is called 'stepping down' your goal. If it is too small to motivate you, you can 'step up' to a bigger goal. Ask 'If I achieved this goal, what would it mean to me?' And step up your target, perhaps by applying an earlier achievement date to the same goal or by raising the goal (wouldn't you like to be fluent in *four* languages rather than one, or compete nationally rather than regionally?) until the idea excites and motivates you.

What else might be affected?

Although it is fine to set and achieve goals in isolation, sometimes one might be in conflict with another or, more commonly, might have some indirect negative effect in another area of your life. Placing an outcome within the wider context of your life, relationships, and the world around you is called an ecology test. For example, gaining a qualification might involve spending a lot of time on your own studying, which might adversely affect your marriage and family relationships, work commitments, existing hobbies, social pursuits and other outside relationships. So the pleasure you stand to gain by achieving the narrow objective is reduced or cancelled by its wider negative implications. You therefore need to reconcile your goals, by asking this *ecology* question. You may then wish to change or postpone some of your goals to create a better overall balance in your life. This presents a great opportunity to work out your real priorities and ensure that the effort you are putting in is being channelled in the best possible way. The questions you need to ask are: 'Who else would this affect?' 'What would happen if I got it?' and 'If I could get it straight away, would I take it?' If your response is 'Yes, but . . .', it probably means there is a problem. And, once again, you can take these doubts into account by changing your original goal.

PUTTING YOUR GOALS IN THE RIGHT ORDER

There is more that you can do at this goal-setting stage to ensure that you will consistently get what you want. This chapter is concerned with how you as a person achieve your goals: the pattern you follow, rather than the content of the specific goals. The approach you will learn involves making sense of your list of goals in the context of your longer-term or 'life' goals, and your own unique personality, priorities and values.

To do or to have?

Start with the list you have already made and, for present purposes, add on another six or seven desires, without thinking them through deeply. Just get down on paper what you want, expressing each desire in your own words. Now, taking each goal or desire in turn, ask yourself the following questions: is the goal about *doing* something — like travelling, doing a training course, or embarking on a new sport or pastime? Or is it about *getting* or *having* something, like a house, a car, a promotion, or perhaps a certificate or award. Note this different emphasis in the goals you have written down. The words you have used will help you determine whether your goal fits into the *doing* or *having/getting* category. Label any goals on your list that fit into these two categories.

We can go further. Is your desire more to do with *knowing* something extra — about an academic subject, about your job, or about a hobby or special interest? Or is it to do with *relating* to people — family, friends or colleagues? Again, label any goals on your list that fit into these categories. Finally, see whether what you want involves *being*: to be your own boss, to *be* slimmer, to *be* more financially secure, to *be* content? This last category is concerned with a state you want to achieve, or the 'place' you want to be in, whether physical, mental or spiritual.

You should now be able to fit all your goals into these five categories: doing, getting/having, knowing, relating and being. (Don't worry for the moment if one goal fits into more than one category — say to *get* a bigger house and thus solve some family *(relating)* problem.) Now consider whether there is a predominance of one or two of the categories. It is common to find such a predominance and this reveals a lot about the way each of us forms our desires and goals.

For example, some people are very concerned with possessions — with *getting* and *having* things. A career advancement for such a person involves *getting* a pay increase, *having* a better car and house, and perhaps *having* a bigger desk and office. Others are more concerned with *doing*. They will 'have a go' at new activities, more concerned with enjoying the *doing* than with what they will *get*. What about *knowing*? Are you the sort of person who has to find out everything there is to know about a product or an activity before committing yourself? If not, you probably know someone like that. Such a person, whilst looking forward to having a new stereo system, will find pleasure in gaining all the knowledge he can before deciding which one to buy. The same person is likely to find out all there is to *know* about a holiday destination, before *doing* the actual travelling. For such a person, *knowing* is important, and will feature strongly in any list of desires. Others will use the *being* words frequently. They want the promotion in order to *be* in charge, or *be* respected; the nest-egg in the bank to *be* independent, the holiday to *be* free or alone, the new furniture to *be* comfortable. When family, friends and work colleagues keep appearing in your list, then *relating* is what is important to you; and this will be reflected in your desires and goals.

Whilst you may have a single, predominant category, or a couple of categories, your list will probably comprise a mixture of some or all of them.

What then?

You should now have put all your goals into one or other of these five categories, and seen whether you have a predominant one. But what you have done reveals much more about yourself, your desires, and how you will achieve them. Try this. Take any one of your goals and ask yourself: 'If I had this, fully and completely, what then?'; and note which of the five categories your answer falls into. For instance, if you are a salesperson you may want to increase your sales by say 50 per cent over the next six months (*doing*). In answer to 'What then?' you might say: 'Well, it's obvious, I will get more commission — more money' (*getting/having*). What then? 'Well, we will get the bigger house we have been hoping for' (another *getting*). What then? 'That will solve the family problems' (*relating*). What then? 'I think I would then be content' (*being*). What then? 'That's it. What more is there? I'd be happy' (*being* again).

So now you have established your personal pattern, how one desire leads to another until you get what you really want. Note the sequence in the above example. *Doing* was followed by *getting*, which was followed by *relating*, which was followed by *being*. Often one category will have more than one interim goal; *getting* money to get a car, or *being* respected in order to *be* happy.

Finally you need to ensure you have identified your *whole* pattern or cycle of desires. Go back to the goal you started with. In the example it was to increase your sales by 50 per cent (*doing*). Then ask: 'Is there anything I need to know, do, get or be, or anyone I need to relate to, in order to achieve this?' The answer might well be: 'I need to have much more product knowledge and more specialist training' (*knowing*). So you now have the following complete cycle:

knowing

doing

getting

relating

being

Life contents

These five categories are described in NLP as 'life contents' and your personal combination, and the order in which each category occurs, is your 'cycle of life contents'. Now ask the same series of questions for several more of your listed goals. Don't forget to go back and ask the final question when you think you have exhausted all the 'What then?' questions.

What should emerge is a repeating pattern — the same life content areas in the same order. This may comprise perhaps three, four or all five, as in the example. And don't be surprised if your order is different from the example. Some people are not concerned about *knowing*. If they are, they might do the *doing* first, such as travel or a new hobby, then get to *know* about the country or activity afterwards. So the order would be *doing*, followed by *knowing*, rather than the other way round. Again, in some cases a person will want to sort out their relationships with others in order to *do* something, whilst another will naturally *do* something in order to achieve the *relating* desire. Often the *being* category is at the end of the cycle, as our deepest desires frequently concern happiness and personal identity, rather than the more tangible goals we associate with achieving those states of being. But we are all different, and sometimes *being* does not even appear.

When you identify your own recurring life content cycle, it will probably feel right and familiar. It is the way you live your life, the way you achieve what you want, the way you express your unique values. It might come as a surprise that other people just as naturally follow a different pattern.

If you think back to times when you have achieved something worthwhile, you will probably be able to spot the same life content cycle in operation. In cases where you have failed to get what you want, you might well find that you did not follow your preferred pattern. People who have to *know* first, for example, will find that when this stage is omitted (for instance, if they are persuaded to do something, or acquire something without the comfort of knowing all there is to know first), they end up feeling dissatisfied with the outcome.

KNOW THYSELF

If you carry out this life content exercise you will learn a lot about yourself. You will be able to clarify your goals, not just one by one, but as a total package. You will learn which types of goals are important to you, and thus which ones on your list are likely to motivate you sufficiently to achieve final success. You will also learn what interim goals have to be fulfilled in order for you to know, do, get, be or relate. You might want to eliminate, adjust or add to the goals you have already listed to take account of what you have learned about yourself. If *having* is important, make sure that at the end of any activity you *have* something tangible. So, for instance, if you are *doing* some study, make sure there is a certificate to *get*. If you are working hard for promotion, make sure there is some*thing* that will provide evidence of your success, and will fulfil your desire to get and have.

If you are not happy with what you have learned about yourself, at least you now know what you need to concentrate on. Maybe you want to be more attuned to *being* – to enjoying each moment regardless of whether you can always *do* what you want or *have* what you want. If this is the case you should look again at each goal. There may be a more direct way to *be* what you want to *be*, without the *doing* and *getting*. After all, you might aspire to a state of mind that has more to do with your beliefs and feelings than the outward achievement of goals. It's easy to end up wasting a lot of years striving for goals that do not give us what we are really looking for.

If you have clarified your goals and identified your personal life content cycle, you have already gone a long way towards getting what you want. You have begun to establish specifically what your goals are, added some common sense and realism, and arranged your many desires in line with your unique personality and priorities. In short, you have begun to answer the question 'What is really important to me?' Having got the answer (and you will then be one of a fortunate minority), you will be able to apply your motivation and resources to getting what you really want.

TAKE ACTION

Now take action. Start making your thoughts reality. Ask the question: 'What do *I* have to *do, now* to ensure that my goal will be fulfilled?' Take the first, most important step — book the course, make the telephone call, buy the magazine — that will set you on the path to success, committing you to fulfil each goal you have set yourself.

3

Knowing How You Feel

▼

WHAT WE DO, WHAT WE ACHIEVE, depends a lot on how we feel. The most insignificant events can knock us for six, and affect our motivation, concentration and productivity. Have you ever experienced that single telephone call that ruins the rest of your day? Or the heavy buff envelope falling on the doormat that seems to spoil everything? It is even more frustrating when you simply don't 'feel' good — not sick, just lethargic and unhappy — and you don't know why. There are some days when you seem to accomplish nothing, and the reason usually boils down to the way you *feel*. Your skills have not diminished overnight and there is no logical reason for such a change in outward behaviour. Conversely, you seem to produce miracles when you feel happy and positive. Nothing has to happen for you to feel good. Your state of mind, or how you feel, is all to do with emotions and thoughts; in particular the thoughts that go on below the surface of your consciousness. Being able to change how you feel, or at least keep some degree of control over your feelings, is therefore bound to affect what you do and what you achieve. Most of us have 'learned' lots of ways to feel bad, and not so many ways to feel good. But you can learn to *choose* how you feel, and this is a large part of what NLP has to offer.

WHAT STATE ARE YOU IN?

However we feel, whatever *state* we are in, we do our best to achieve what we want to achieve. That is, we are always goal-directed, we still want to succeed in our outcomes, even if we are hampered by our state of mind. Our state might be unresourceful, or disempowering, so we do not achieve the result we are after. A state can be defined as all the millions of neurological processes happening in our brain at any time — what we might also call our experience. Most of these states happen without our ever being conscious of them. We don't usually consciously decide to be frustrated or envious or upset, in the way that we decide we are going to make a telephone call or calculate a discount. Nevertheless, our brain chemistry changes, as does the rest of our physiology, as we move from state to state. We are always in some state, and that state always affects our behaviour.

Just stopping to think about the state you are in, putting a name to it, and holding an 'inner dialogue' can immediately change how you feel. Let's say you are angry. The message getting to your brain is probably that some rule or value you hold dear has been broken by someone. Knowing that our maps of the world differ so much (one of the first principles of NLP), this is bound to happen from time to time. We are all the products of different environments and experiences, and have different intentions, however we seek to fulfil them. Perhaps people unknowingly do things that cause you to be angry. So maybe your anger stems from *your* choice to apply *your* rules and values to other people. Or you may be angry with yourself, in which case you may be able to identify the 'rules' you have broken or standards you have missed that have brought about this feeling. (Having identified these 'rules', you will then be free to challenge them.)

The common emotion of disappointment is probably a feeling of being let down, or failing to achieve a goal you had hoped for, sometimes because the goal itself is inappropriate or badly expressed. The goal clarification exercise in Chapter 2 helps you avoid such disappointments. And the principle 'There is no failure, only feedback' will help you to see things in a different light. Perhaps you have been too dependent on others, or you may not have done the 'ecology' check that puts what you want in the context of other goals, and other parts of your life. What can you learn from your disappointment? Maybe another angle will present itself or other, more fulfilling, goals might be born out of the experience. Any feeling or state can be 'put in a box', and seen in a more objective light. Bear in mind that a state is a *resource*. Like anger or frustration, it has a positive use in some contexts. You can decide whether how you feel is empowering or disempowering, and, using the techniques described in this chapter, you can make a choice.

HOW YOUR FEELINGS AFFECT YOU

Usually we react to events in an emotional, irrational way. Consider two workers, both fairly competent. They hear that the boss is coming over in five minutes to review their work. George immediately becomes frightened, perhaps imagining being embarrassed or reprimanded, demoted or even fired, wondering about the 'hidden agenda' behind the boss's visit. As the seconds go by, he goes into a state of mild panic, imagining how his family and friends would react if he lost his job, and how difficult it would be to find another one. No income! Danger! Terror! Papers fly round his desk and files are stacked away as he is works out ingenious excuses for why he is so far behind on a couple of tasks.

Meanwhile Bill, his colleague, on hearing of the review welcomes his boss's interest. He welcomes the chance to impress, raise a couple of questions, and perhaps take the opportunity to ask for a pay rise. He has a rising sense of excitement and pleasure as he looks forward to the boss's arrival.

What is happening? The same outward sensual stimuli are interpreted very differently by each worker. Each filters his thoughts in a certain way, so that a different 'message' reaches his brain, to give a certain understanding of the situation. And it is this filtered interpretation that creates the state that dramatically changes the behaviour, and no doubt the actual results, of the two workers' reviews.

Now what exactly happened to George when his brain picked up these unhappy thoughts? As the largest gland in the body, the brain has a tremendous impact on all our other organs, systems, tissues and cells. George's fear was picked up by the hypothalamus, the great 'pilot' of the brain which controls so many other functions. The hypothalamus immediately triggered an adrenalin rush throughout his bloodstream. In less than a second the message of the boss's visit turned poor George's body chemistry upside down, as powerful chemicals flooded his system. His bronchial tubes were jacked open for deeper breathing. His heart beat faster and contracted more strongly. His blood pressure rose. Sugar poured into his bloodstream for extra energy. The digestive system shut down. The blood vessels in his skin contracted, slowing the flow of blood (turning him pale). His eyes dilated so he could see better. The blood vessels in his muscles opened wider, allowing more blood to flow through the muscles. The muscles themselves contracted (making him feel tense).

If you 'feel' for George as you read, you are undergoing a milder version of all this right now! This is what is called stress. It was caused, quite simply, by how George *thought* about a situation; what *he* did in *his* brain. He was, literally, in a state. And this state fundamentally affected his whole physiology, and his behaviour. With a few repetitions, his health would deteriorate. And in the longer term, with that sort of reaction to similar events, he is unlikely to get a good return on his pension contributions.

These sorts of reactions are useful, sometimes vital, in the right context. If you are faced with a mugger at night, all those instant physiological changes will do wonders for your ability to fight or flee. But nowadays they are rarely needed in such life or death situations. Instead they place our bodies and immune systems under great stress, resulting in numerous psychosomatic complaints that combine to stop us achieving our outcomes.

The techniques of NLP allow us to take control of our states — our feelings. They give us choices. If you think anger is appropriate to achieve an outcome, then you can choose that state. But you have the choice. Many of us have already experienced changing our state on certain occasions. Some people can psych themselves up, or have mental tricks they use to make themselves feel better. Or they resort to certain behaviour, like going for a fast run or cleaning the car. But these happen more by default than design and we do not understand them enough to apply them to other, perhaps more important, situations we face. So NLP takes a skill that many of us know about at some level, and others use frequently to great effect, and makes it constantly available to everyone. Getting results depends on what you do. The big variable affecting what you do is the state you are in, how you feel, and what you believe about yourself and the situation. All this can now be placed under your control.

What causes these feelings, which were so different in the case of George and Bill? What are the processes going on inside? To understand this, we need to find a way of understanding our own thought processes.

TAKING CONTROL OF YOUR MIND

When we think about what we see, hear and feel, we use these same senses inwardly. What George and Bill experienced were inner representations in the form of visual, auditory and kinesthetic senses — a mirror of the way we interpret the objective, outer world. We call these *representation systems*, or *modalities*. Including taste and smell, all five are represented internally, although we use the main three — seeing, hearing and feeling — most, in that order. Not surprisingly, the pictures, sounds and feelings going through the minds of each worker were very different. And this difference created their different states of mind.

We each have a preference for which sense we use, for the way we think. Some people are happier with images and pictures, rather than sounds. For example, if I ask you to describe what you are experiencing as you read, would you start by describing what you can see, or the sounds, or the feelings? And which would you give the most attention to in your description? People we describe as 'kinesthetic' are very aware of physical sensations, and are more likely to describe the feel of the chair they are sitting on than the traffic noise down the street, or the sunlight on the page. We give clues to our preference by using particular words and phrases. 'I get the picture' or 'I see what you are saying' indicate a visual preference. 'I hear what you say' or 'That sounds good' suggest an auditory preference. Whereas 'It feels right' or 'I can grasp that idea' are the sort of phrases you would hear from people with a kinesthetic preference.

This thinking preference is likely to reflect an actual sensual preference — which sense you prefer to use when taking in and relating to the outside world. Some people easily remember faces (visual) whilst others remember names (usually by the sound, auditory). Some people like to consider a problem by drawing pictures, or using diagrams or symbols other than words. Others like to talk a problem through, perhaps writing down a list of the pros and cons but inwardly 'hearing' what is written. Some people are good listeners, whilst others are very observant in a visual way. Others detect subtle feelings, and might well use body language to 'touch' people. In a buying situation, some of us are happy to listen, others like to see, and others are not content until they have felt or handled the product. In fact we use all our senses to different degrees, but it is common to have a preference.

You may not have thought about all this before, in which case you may not know what your preference is, but this will soon become apparent. The fact is that we are too busy thinking to think about it! We just *think*, without being aware of the *process*, even though we are doing it all the time with great skill. So it is no surprise that we do not know how *others* think, and tend to assume that they think the same way as we do — that, given the same facts and arguments, they are eventually bound to see it our way. But this is not the case. As we saw in the first chapter we each have our own maps of reality. And one of the things that makes us very different is our thinking preference — which senses we prefer to use inwardly.

USING YOUR INNER SENSES

Let us stop for a moment to experiment with our inner senses. Read the next paragraph carefully.

You are walking slowly along a deserted beach. The sun is hot on your body, and you can feel the texture of the warm sand on your bare feet. Somewhere in the distance you hear children laughing, then the shrill call of gulls circling just ahead. The sun's reflection on the water makes you squint, and you are relaxed by the constant gentle lapping of the small waves. Your head feels light. You feel the tiniest of breezes on your body. A motorcycle screams off along the coast road.

To make any sense of this paragraph, you had to see, hear and feel things inwardly, even though you were not aware of what you were doing, just of the experience you were creating. This is how we *understand*, how words come to life in our experience. Because you were guided through the experience, you probably used all three main representation systems, although you may have had more difficulty in imagining one or two, whilst another sense was very easy to create, and more vivid.

When you are reading an exciting novel, you are using all your thinking ability in a natural way, constantly creating the inner pictures, sounds and feelings that the words evoke. As you become unconscious of what is going on immediately around you — although you are wide awake and all your outward senses are functioning — these inner representation systems become predominant. For a while at least, your world is the inner subjective one of the novel. You have escaped, if you like, from objective reality. But consider this. If the writer is a strongly kinesthetic person, thinking and writing in feeling terms, and you are a visualising person, you will be on different wavelengths. (At least this is how, using the word 'wavelengths', an auditory person might describe it.) The necessary *rapport* between writer and reader will not be established. And this is not so much to do with writing style, or even skill, but personal sensory preference.

The same applies to spoken communication. You can like someone because their way of speaking mirrors your own thinking preference. You might describe him or her as 'my kind of person'. Even if your own preference is different, knowing their preference and understanding how this can be used to achieve rapport (by making the necessary changes in what you say and how you say it) can help you become very influential in your dealings with others.

IDENTIFYING YOUR OWN THINKING PREFERENCE

You can easily do a rough check on your own preference by following this exercise which requires you to think visually, auditorily and kinesthetically. For each item you recall or imagine, give yourself a score between 1 and 9. A top score of 9 means you can easily represent inwardly what is asked — a picture would be very clear and in focus, for example, or a feeling would be almost like in real life. If you struggle to make any representation at all, score a minimum 1. Then use the rest of the scale to indicate how easy (high score) or hard (low score) it is to conjure up the memory or imagination. Don't spend too long on each one; if you need to spend a long time conjuring up an inner sense it means you should mark that one low. Do not record any answers, just circle a number on the scale at the end. There are six examples for each of the three main modalities.

Visual

1. Which of your friends or relations has the longest hair?

2. Recall the face of a teacher from when you were at school.

3. Visualise the stripes on a tiger.

4. See the colour of the front door where you live or work.

5. See a favourite entertainer on your TV screen wearing a top hat.

6. Visualise the largest book in your house.

Auditory

1. Hear a favourite tune.

2. Listen to church bells ringing in the distance.

3. Which of your friends has the quietest voice?

4. Hear a car engine starting on a cold morning.

5. Imagine hearing the voice of a childhood friend.

6. Listen to the sound your voice makes under water.

Kinesthetic

1. Feel your left hand in very cold water.

2. Hold a smooth, glass paperweight in both hands.

3. Stroke a cat or dog.

4. Put on a pair of wet socks.

5. Imagine jumping off a four-foot-high wall.

6. Roll a car wheel down the road.

Visual

1.	1	2	3	4	5	6	7	8	9
2.	1	2	3	4	5	6	7	8	9
3.	1	2	3	4	5	6	7	8	9
4.	1	2	3	4	5	6	7	8	9
5.	1	2	3	4	5	6	7	8	9
6.	1	2	3	4	5	6	7	8	9

Average visual rating _____

Auditory

1.	1	2	3	4	5	6	7	8	9
2.	1	2	3	4	5	6	7	8	9
3.	1	2	3	4	5	6	7	8	9
4.	1	2	3	4	5	6	7	8	9
5.	1	2	3	4	5	6	7	8	9
6.	1	2	3	4	5	6	7	8	9

Average auditory rating _____

Kinesthetic

1.	1	2	3	4	5	6	7	8	9
2.	1	2	3	4	5	6	7	8	9
3.	1	2	3	4	5	6	7	8	9
4.	1	2	3	4	5	6	7	8	9
5.	1	2	3	4	5	6	7	8	9
6.	1	2	3	4	5	6	7	8	9

Average kinesthetic rating _____

Now add up your total score for each of the three modalities, and divide by six to work out an average for each. Notice whether one of the three categories gives you a higher score than the other two, or whether one is significantly lower than the other two. If you want to make your preference score more accurate — although it is just your subjective scoring — you can think of some more examples yourself.

IDENTIFYING OTHER PEOPLE'S THINKING PREFERENCES

You can easily determine someone else's preference. Without letting them know what you are up to, make a mental note of all the words and figures of speech that suggest a seeing, hearing or feeling preference. Such words and phrases, or *predicates*, are used so frequently that we usually do not notice them. Some of the expressions only make sense when you realise that the person is revealing their particular preference. 'I see what you are saying' does not make as much sense as 'I hear what you are saying', until we realise that the person interprets what is said by putting it into internal images, or pictures. It is then what he or she *sees* that makes sense. In a twenty-minute conversation many such clues are likely to *appear* (note that I have used the visual word 'appear', which betrays the fact that I am happy in visual mode). Where there is a predominance of one kind of phrase, a preference is likely. Sometimes two might crop up frequently (perhaps feeling and seeing), but the third (hearing) is conspicuous (note again the visual expression!) by its absence. It is not so easy to be sure of your own preference using figures of speech unless you can call upon a friend to do the same exercise with you.

Language cues

Here are a few sensory-based words and phrases, both to illustrate just how common they are, and to act as a checklist for you to determine someone else's preference. If it *sounds* like a lot of trouble, we shall shortly *see* how you can *feel* the benefit of this knowledge, both as it applies to yourself and also to others.

Words

- **Visual**: picture, bright, colour, look, black, vision, eye, scene, vivid, visualise, imagine, reveal, reflect, clarify, insight, perspective, notice, see, dark, hazy, focus, shine.

- **Auditory**: loud, ring, clear, discuss, tell, quiet, say, hear, ask, remark, click, hearsay, harmony, deaf, tune, dumb, call, rhythm, sound, wave-length.

- **Kinesthetic**: touch, push, solid, scrape, heavy, rough, smooth, contact, move, pressure, handle, thrust, grasp, weight, rub, sticky, warm, cold, tackle, firm, tangible.

- **Olfactory (smell)**: stale, nosy, fresh, whiff, stink, fishy.

- **Gustatory (taste)**: sweet, sour, flavour, bitter, taste, chew, swallow, bite.

- **Neutral (non-sensory-based)**: sense, think, know, notice, understand, explain, decide, learn, change, recognise, perceive, remember, arrange.

Phrases:

- **Visual**: 'I see what you mean', 'a blind spot', 'it appears', 'you'll look back on this', 'show me', 'eye to eye', 'mind's eye', 'sight for sore eyes', 'looking closely', 'hazy notion', 'shed some light'.

- **Auditory**: 'in a manner of speaking', 'turn a deaf ear', 'rings a bell', 'word for word', 'hold your tongue', 'loud and clear', 'on the same wavelength', 'unheard of ', 'calling the tune', 'makes him/her tick'.

- **Kinesthetic**: 'hold on a second', 'cool customer', 'warm-hearted person', 'thick skinned', 'I can grasp that idea', 'heated argument', 'smooth operator', 'I can't put my finger on it', 'scratch the surface', 'I feel it in my bones', 'I will be in touch', 'turns me on'.

- **Olfactory and gustatory**: 'smell a rat', 'bitter pill', 'fresh as a daisy', 'acid comment', 'that will go down well', 'swallow that', 'matter of taste', 'one man's meat'.

These are some of the predicate cues to the representation systems that others are using. If one of these categories sounds very familiar to you, and you can imagine yourself using the words, it probably confirms that this is your preferred representation system.

Body language cues

Words and phrases are not the only way we can determine a person's thinking preference. A person who thinks visually will usually speak quickly, with the head up, and using a higher pitch than an auditory person, who will tend to breathe and speak in a more rhythmic, clear and resonant tone. People who are 'talking to themselves' are likely to lean their head to one side, in a typical listening position — as though holding a telephone conversation. A kinesthetic person is likely to speak in a slow, deeper tone, relaxed and with the head down. Although these 'rules' may not always hold true, as you start observing people and matching what they say to their posture and tone of voice, you will see just how often these mannerisms are apparent. So, as well as verbal cues, or predicates, there are also physiological, or body language cues to thinking preference.

Eye movement cues

Another form of cue, which many people new to NLP find the most fascinating of all, is in the way we move our eyes when thinking. If I ask you to visualise the face of a schoolteacher, as far back as you can remember, you will probably look slightly up and to your left. If I ask you to remember his or her voice, or perhaps the sound of the bell or buzzer signalling the end of a class, you will probably move your eyes to the left, but not up or down. But if you are asked to remember the feeling of the surface of your school desk, or the feel of the soap in your hand in the school washroom, or any other past kinesthetic experience, you will probably, without being aware of it, look down and to your right. The diagram on page 58 shows what these eye movements look like if you are facing the person. The patterns may be reversed for some left-handed people.

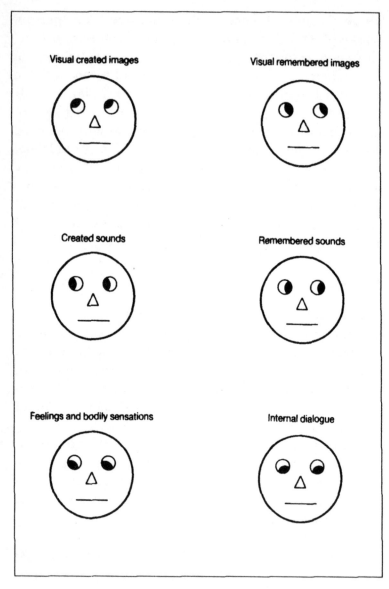

Pattern of eye movements

All this is to do with accessing different parts of the brain when we think. It is well researched and is referred to as 'lateral eye movements' in neurological literature. In NLP these eye movements are known as *eye accessing cues*. Along with the predicates and body language cues we have just discussed, they can help us determine which thinking sense is being used.

Let us say you have to think of a visual image which is *not* stored in your memory. When visualising a fantastic or bizarre *constructed* image, whilst still looking slightly upwards, you would probably look to the right rather than the left. For a constructed sound — like an imaginary hen clucking an imaginary version of your favourite melody — rather than a remembered one, your eyes would move to the right, but not up or down. When we conduct inner dialogue, the sort of internal running conversation which most people are familiar with, the eye movement is different again, and involves looking down and to our left.

Of course, you are free to look anywhere you like when you are thinking, and if you are conscious of what you are doing you may not follow the patterns I have described. So start checking this out by watching other people who are not aware of what is happening. In seminars a single delegate, unaware of what is going on, is asked to recall memories and imagine different thoughts. During a short conversation the person may use literally hundreds of eye movements, watched in some amazement by the other delegates. The subject is completely unaware of his or her eye movements. But you will need to develop your own skill in watching for cues, as movements are often very fast. This is because we think fast, especially in visual mode.

As well as the problem of speed, our thinking

preference means that our thoughts do not always follow any 'logical' pattern. So, for instance, a person with a strong recollection of sounds will easily recall the voice, and probably the actual words, of a schoolteacher or an old friend. When asked to visualise the person, the auditory thinker might first have to hear the memory, and then switch to the image, and so on to recall feelings. In other words, we each have a preferred way to enter a memory recording. We think the way we want to think, even if this is in a roundabout way. So, in watching the eyes, this actual sequence will quickly appear, even though it is contrary to the request to 'visualise'. By asking, 'What did you do when you recalled that memory?' you will often be able to make sense of eye movements, and also spot a recurring preference for memory recall.

LEAD SYSTEMS

This preferred means of bringing memories into conscious thought is called our *lead system*, the internal sense we use to 'lead' us to a mind recording, or memory. However, this lead system is not necessarily the same as our preferred representation system for conscious thinking. So, for example, you may be a 'feeling person' who thinks about a holiday experience in terms of feelings. This is confirmed by the words you use and your body language. But, in recalling a memory, you may first use a *visual* image, which is then replaced by the comfortable kinesthetic sensing you are more at home with. So we each have a preferred representation system, and also a lead system, which may or may not be the same. But the good news is that we tend to be *consistent* in whatever way we think. Whether right- or left-handed, and whatever your mixture of thinking preference, your eye patterns will tend to be the same. So it is well worth understanding your own preference, and the preferences of partners, friends and colleagues you are in contact with a lot, as they will tend to remain the same.

Before you start translating this knowledge into actual benefits, have some fun watching and listening. Develop the skills that tell you how a person is thinking and feeling, and the sort of words and body language that make them warm (note that 'warm' is a kinesthetic predicate) towards you. This sort of rapport is the basis of good communication, of influencing others, and getting what you want.

TUNING IN TO YOUR 'INNER PICTURE'

So far we have considered the main modalities that constitute thought patterns, and our preferences. But that is not enough if we are to understand the important differences that account for such wide variations in the way we feel about things. What caused such variations in the case of George and Bill, for example?

Try an exercise to see for yourself what happens. Think back to a time when you were in a highly 'empowered' state of mind. You achieved some goal, or maybe heard some good news, and felt on top of the world. As you recall the experience, you will be able to see images associated with the memory, hear sounds including any voices, and also relive the feelings — the actual state of mind you were in. Explore each of the main modalities — the sights, sounds and feelings — one at a time. Then combine them to make the experience as real as possible. Right now, you will experience the same feelings you felt then — perhaps a sense of ecstasy, pride, calmness or whatever you experienced. And the more vividly you can recreate your memory, the more your present state will change. If someone is watching you, they will notice changes in your physiology. Your body posture will probably alter, your breathing rate will change, as will your facial expression and even the colour of your skin. All this is apart from the numerous internal changes that cannot be observed — in this case generating pleasant endomorphins instead of the harmful toxins that an unpleasant state produces.

So, from this exercise you have seen that a memory, or thought process, is made up of the same senses you use to understand the outside world. They simply accessed the brain directly rather than via the outer sense organs. You might like to add taste and smell to your list, by recalling an incident involving these two modalities, which, as it happens, are very powerful senses in recalling even distant memories. You have also seen that you can change your present state by simply thinking — remembering or imagining.

CHOOSING HOW YOU FEEL

You can choose whatever state you wish. Maybe you wish to feel complete calmness and peace, in which case you could recall some peaceful holiday retreat, or a place from your past that you associate with calmness and security. If not, you can imagine a fictitious place, your ideal special place amidst glorious landscape and in beautiful weather. This visualisation will change your state in the same way.

As far as your brain is concerned, what you are *thinking* has become your reality. The same modalities are used, the same neurological connections are made, and the same physiological result occurs. Try visualising winning some award or accolade you have only dreamed about, or fulfilling one of your top goals, and just feel what it is like to go through that experience. The human brain does not differentiate between actual sensual stimuli from the outside world and clear internal representations — they are both recorded and acted upon in the same way. This is why, on waking from a vivid dream, you are not certain, for a few moments, which is real — the dream or the room you find yourself in. Similarly, when daydreaming, your reality is where the daydreaming takes you, not the boring lecture hall where you are physically sitting.

Now try something else. Think of another experience from the past, a memory you find easy to recall. Wait until you have a clear image of the situation. You will need to get into a relaxed state to do this. Now make the images bigger and brighter, and focus them clearly. If you can see yourself in the picture, put yourself inside, so that you see things as if through your own eyes. Now make the sounds louder and clearer, and make any voices ones that you are happy with. Make the whole experience fully three-dimensional and larger than life. Bring anything in the distance near. Then check how you feel. If you have someone with you they will be able to see any changes in your physiology. You will probably feel even better than you did when just recalling the memory in whatever way it came to you. Pleasant, empowering experiences are usually represented clearly and brightly, and, especially as if seen through your own eyes, you are right there enjoying it.

This last distinction is very important. When you visualise yourself in a particular situation you can either look through your own eyes, or you can see yourself as someone else might see you. These two ways of seeing are termed 'associated' and 'dissociated'. In real life, of course, our view of the world is always associated.

If you do more of these recollections you will find that a visual image can be very bright or quite dull, larger than life or small and distant, in black and white or colour — much like the adjustments you can make to a television picture. These variations are termed *submodalities*. In the same way, sounds can have different characteristics, as can feelings. In your happy imaging you will tend to feel happy, and in your distasteful visualisation you will tend to feel bad, just as you do in real life. It might be that in your happy recollection, your image is associated (seen through your own eyes), whereas in a painful, negative memory you might see yourself from outside, even from a distance. Check this out.

As you compare the differences between your positive and negative memories or visualisation (you can imagine some future event) you will start to see a pattern of submodalities. In simple terms, some characteristics will be associated with pleasurable images, and some will be associated with painful images — whatever the actual content of the scenes. Looked at in this way, it is easier to understand how one person's delight is another person's terror; we each construct very different inner maps of the same outward event or situation. That is, we perceive things differently. And this unique package of submodalities determines how we feel about something, how we see ourselves, our attitudes, beliefs, hang-ups and phobias.

For the moment just try to get familiar with entering your inner, subjective world and exploring the differences in the submodalities. As with any skill, it will take time and practice to become comfortable doing this. Start with recent memories you can easily recapture. It will be worth the effort. You should then include some unpleasant memories, so that you can easily compare the different characteristics, or submodalities, in these and pleasant memories. In the case of painful representations, it is more common for images to be small, distant and unfocused, and for sounds to be less clear. In particular, unpleasant associations will often be dissociated — you will be outside the scene, watching it as an observer. It is this unique combination of submodalities that constitutes, for you, a pleasurable or a painful representation, and determines the state you are in; literally, how you feel. You now have an understanding of, and also access to how you think at a subconscious level to create varying states of mind.

The next stage is to *change* the submodalities, one by one, and thus literally change any representation you make of a memory, a future event, or a belief about something. Having recognised what, for you, are empowering submodalities — the detailed characteristics which form a recurring pattern in positive, empowering states — all that remains is for you to replace the disempowering submodalities with the empowering ones, one by one. The list overleaf shows which common submodalities you can use as a checklist. Don't worry if some don't apply or seem silly. Just try and spot any differences, and make a note of them.

CHECKLIST OF SUBMODALITIES

Visual

Associated or dissociated
Colour or black and white
Location (e.g., to the left or right, up or down)
Distance
Brightness
Framed or panoramic
Blurred or focused
Contrast
Moving or still
Speed (faster or slower than real life)
Size

Auditory

Loud or soft
Distance from sound source
Words or sounds
Location of sound source
Stereo or mono
Continuous or discontinuous
Speed (faster or slower than usual)
Clear or muffled
Soft or harsh

Kinesthetic (feeling)

Temperature
Texture (rough or smooth)
Intensity

Pressure (hard or soft)
Duration (how long it lasts)
Weight (light or heavy)
Shape

At this point we need a practical exercise demonstrating how to recognise and change these submodalities. But first we need to put ourselves in the right frame of mind.

THE ALPHA STATE

The mind visualises best when you are in a relaxed state of mind, without the pressure of the objective, conscious world around you. The period just before going off to sleep, for instance, is associated with slow brainwaves known as alpha, and this is a very receptive time to do anything subjectively — remembering, imagining or manipulating thoughts. It is similar to a daydreaming state. Although the body is relaxed, the mind is alert and open to suggestion. So you should get into a relaxed state, and there are plenty of ways to do this. I have listed some helpful books under Further Reading.

Here is a useful technique based on visualising descending numbers. Go through a basic relaxation exercise, feeling each limb getting heavier, then including your neck, face and eyes. Now count downwards from 100 to 1 slowly. Keep your breathing slow. Repeat and visualise the final numbers 3, 2 and 1 several times, and make them *memorable* in some way — using a particular colour or type face, or even a bizarre representation of the number. Also make them *dynamic* in some way — for instance picture yourself writing the numbers with a special pen, maybe on your bedroom wall, or keying them onto an imaginary computer screen. Try to incorporate sights, sounds and feelings. You will now always associate those numbers, portrayed in your special way, with the state of deep relaxation you achieve during these exercises.

Let 3 represent full physical relaxation, so don't visualise the number 3 until you feel you have reached that state. Number 2 will represent mental relaxation, when you have eliminated 'busy thoughts' and awareness of your objective surroundings. And number 1, the deepest state you can achieve from which you can create subjective outcomes. This simple descending sequence of numbers is your door to a whole new inner, subjective world, and effort put into this practice will be repaid many times over. Once you are in a dreamy yet highly aware alpha state of mind, you are ready to do this sort of exercise. Make sure you will not be interrupted for a while.

CHANGING SUBMODALITIES

Let us use attending a job interview as an illustration of how to recognise and change submodalities. Let's say that this experience is not pleasant for you, and it is one in which you want to increase your confidence. The very thought of it fills you with foreboding, and you are sure that your performance in the past has not done justice to your experience and abilities. If you have no difficulty with interviews, then choose something else — it might be sitting examinations, meeting new people, moving house, or whatever, and follow the same procedure. It is best if you can think back to an actual memory, as it is easier to visualise a real experience, and the association of the actual interview you recall probably accounts to some extent for the negative way you feel now.

Now relive your interview (or other difficult experience) by going successively through each modality, the sights, sounds, feelings, and — where applicable — tastes and smells. What does the chair feel like? What does the carpet feel like on the soles of your feet? All these sensations are recorded somewhere on the hard disk of your memory. As you dwell on the experience, in a relaxed state, you may be surprised at how many details you can recall. This part of the exercise may not be pleasant, but you can remind yourself that this could change how you feel about interviews once and for all, so a small investment of discomfort is well worth it

Using the submodality checklist on pages 66/7, identify as many as possible. How do the voices compare with real life — are they faster or slower, clear or muffled, pleasing or sinister? What about other sounds, from other offices or outside the building? Are you in the picture as seen from outside, and if so from which position — above, behind, in front? Are you in the distance, smaller than real life, or large? How about the colours? Are they bright, or dull — even black and white or sepia like an old photograph? And is the overall picture as if on a video or cinema screen, or panoramic so you can see 360 degrees around? Make a note of any submodalities you can identify, and how you feel. You may have to spend a little time on this. You may also need to think of another interview experience you can recall more vividly (even though it is not your worst interview) in which it is easier to visualise this sort of detail — perhaps a more recent occasion.

Then go through the same exercise for an experience you recall with pleasure, in which you were masterly and confident (which for someone else might well be a job interview). Let's say it is playing badminton and winning at a local event. Maybe these images are bigger and brighter, with loud, clear sound, and seen through your own eyes. However they differ, switch each submodality, one by one, until you can relive the interview with all the same thinking characteristics, or submodalities, of the badminton victory. And notice how you feel. Has the painful anxiety of the interview been replaced by the nervous excitement and pleasure of the badminton victory?

It is worth persevering at this as you are changing your state of mind about the experience in question once and for all. Do some mental rehearsal, what is termed *future pacing* — imagine attending another interview for a job — to check what effect the changes have had. Enjoy the experience, just as you might enjoy the anticipation of going to stay with a favourite friend, going off to a special holiday retreat, or a celebration dinner. Your feelings about job interviews have changed, because you have changed the actual neural connections in the brain that create the feelings. Then be ready to put your new confidence into practice at the first available opportunity. Why not try for a job that seems well out of your league and see what happens?

In this chapter you have learned how feelings affect what we do and achieve, and how those feelings, and other thought processes are formed by inner representations of the five outer senses. You have begun to explore your subjective, inner world and learn how to change what goes on inside. Now you can begin to take control, and use your thoughts to support you in bringing about your chosen outcomes.

4

Would You Believe It?

▼

OUR FEELINGS CHANGE FREQUENTLY throughout the day, as we are exposed to events, circumstances and people that cause us to react in different ways. A single casual comment or minor event can make us feel bad. Often our changes in state are short-lived, and meeting a different person, glancing at our watch and seeing that there is only ten minutes to go, or getting absorbed in a favourite television programme can get us back on form. But we can just as quickly change back to an unresourceful state. Once we understand that these swings in state and behaviour are the result of how we *think*, and that we can decide what we think (nobody can make you unhappy if you really don't want to be), we can start to give ourselves choices. We can decide what is the most empowering state to help us achieve our outcomes and feel what we want to feel about a situation. This level of control over how we feel takes a bit of skill and practice — but no more than any of the complex physical skills that you and I carry out without thinking. Even without a high level of subjective skill, your new understanding of the process gives everything a new objectivity. Your state is no longer an autocratic master, dictating your every move. By changing your state, consciously and wilfully, in the last chapter, you demonstrated that such control was possible.

HABITS OF THOUGHT

More deeply rooted feelings develop into thought habits, or *attitudes*, that are far more restricting than feelings that come and go. Being 'positive' or 'negative', or 'optimistic' or 'pessimistic', displays an attitude. It has long been proven that an optimistic salesperson will outperform a pessimistic salesperson of similar experience and training. I suppose this is common sense. But what is important is that a pessimistic attitude can be changed — and, like our state of mind, is just a matter of how we *think* about things. A change of attitude, without any apparent change in skills or behaviour, can result in quantum improvements in performance.

Research with optimists and pessimists also shows that the gap in output increases over time. A 20 per cent sales lead on the part of the optimists became over 50 per cent the following year. In other words, the law of diminishing returns was reversed, and a positive attitude resulted in an upward spiral of success. Meanwhile those who expected poor results, the pessimists, experienced a downward spiral. The way we think is just as likely to become habitual as the way we act. The attitudes that direct us as individuals and cultures are simply habits of thought that can be changed — with awareness and the right kind of mental practice. Lionel Tiger's book *Optimism* demonstrates that cultures that endure are those with optimistic belief systems. Such groups believe in the worth, value and possibilities of their own futures.

SELF-BELIEFS

At a deeper level of thinking we each have our own *beliefs* and *values*. These are far more permanent than ephemeral feelings, or even attitudes. The beliefs that affect what you achieve mostly concern what you believe about yourself, or how you 'see' yourself — your self-image, if you like. A belief that says 'I'm no good when it comes to selling' or 'I'm no good in front of a large group' might be severely limiting, depending on what you want to achieve. A single positive self-belief such as 'I relate well to people' is probably equivalent to many hours of skill training which, without that empowering belief, would only have a short-term effect. On the other hand, a single negative self-belief (like, 'I'm no good with numbers') will effectively cancel out many hours of training and conscious effort; the belief will tend to win the day, like a self-fulfilling prophecy. Each self-belief tends to be supported by a few specific beliefs, or *references*. 'I relate well to people' might be supported by the beliefs: 'I can easily start up a conversation'; 'I am at ease with strangers'; or 'I get on well with so-and so and so-and-so.' The more references that support a belief, the stronger that belief will be.

Extensive research in the USA among schoolchildren showed remarkable changes in academic results based on what the children were led to believe about the colour of their eyes! It does not seem to matter whether the belief has been adopted from an authority figure or a peer, whether it seems rational or irrational, or whether its origin is known or unknown. Once we believe something, and we all believe all sorts of things, our behaviour is affected at every level. What we then believe about our *behaviour* — or, how we interpret it — further affects future behaviour. We are locked into a cycle of beliefs and actions.

The inner you

A lot of writers, sportspeople and business leaders have remarked on how our self-image can affect everything we try to do. Some say it is the single most important factor in all human achievement. Dr Maxwell Maltz, a famous plastic surgeon, found that some patients experienced major personality changes following cosmetic surgery. However, in other cases, even dramatic surgery had no effect on the real problem, and patients still 'saw themselves' as ugly or incompetent. Their inner image of themselves, their *beliefs* about themselves, remained unchanged. By getting them to make changes in their attitude to themselves, rather than their physical bodies, Dr Maltz was able to show outstanding results. NLP offers techniques to change belief systems, including the all-important self-image.

Pathways in the brain

Remember that every experience of your lifetime is stored away in your brain — everything you have ever seen, heard, felt, tasted or smelled. How you perceive each of these memories creates patterns of neural connections — pathways in your brain — that become, with further use, like communication roads and eventually great highways. These recurring, convenient, familiar ways of filtering the new information coming to your brain form your *beliefs*.

For example, if you say 'I can't remember names' that is just your way of interpreting your present experience — perhaps a one-off memory lapse — based in turn on the way you have come to interpret it in the past. In one sense it is absolutely true, and the test of this kind of 'truth' is that you *believe* it to be true. In another sense it is just the way you happen to handle 'remembering names' based upon your accumulated experience. Another person might say 'I can't remember faces'. Both of you have your own personal maps of reality. Neither of you has experienced the real world — everything you understand and believe has come through your perceptual filters. You just made a different 'connection' some time ago and this gradually grew into an efficient, high-speed system for handling the vast array of data you are confronted with moment by moment — you created your own belief. In an objective test, it might be found that you can actually remember names better than your colleague, and that she can remember faces better than you! So beliefs have little to do with objective facts. And if facts do support a belief, which is, thankfully, more normal, this is usually the result of behaviour *confirming belief* in a self-fulfilling way.

So your beliefs consistently filter communications from outside and inside yourself. Along with your feelings, they rule every part of your behaviour, but at a deeper and more consistent level. You literally cannot achieve anything unless your beliefs match your desired outcomes. You will act out what you think, reflecting the state you are in and what you believe. As Virgil wrote: 'They can because they think they can.'

Where do beliefs come from?

Where do these beliefs come from? We have all been subject to different environments in our formative years, and this is an important factor. If you grew up encouraged to believe that you could achieve a lot, this has probably become part of your belief system, and has resulted in what you are today. We all have role models in childhood, and these are a source of self-belief. If you can picture yourself as someone, you start to believe you can be like that person. Thousands of leading sportspeople, performers and businesspeople trace their success back to some early role model. Even a restricting childhood can be affected by a single schoolteacher, relative or mentor who turns the tide of self-belief and sets us on an empowered, worthwhile path through life. Real hardship is not just the daily fight for survival. Many people learn to cope well with whatever environment they are in. The greatest human pain comes from not *believing* there is a future, not being able to dream about something better. That is what an environment can do.

A study was carried out by Dr Benjamin Bloom at the University of Chicago involving successful young athletes, musicians and students. He was surprised to find that most of these young people did not start out with some obvious talent or apparent innate skill. Most had received careful attention as they grew up. Their belief in themselves *preceded* any signs of great talent. If such talent was latent, then something in their environment created the belief system that unlocked their potential. And this is the very process that NLP has identified. Our innate potential, whatever the impact of genetics, is more or less unlimited. And this potential can be unlocked by the way we think.

Circumstances, big and small, will also affect our beliefs. There are some events in your life you will never forget. Another person's experience will be different, even after sharing a similar environment. A different teacher at school often marks the start of a lifelong interest in a subject, and even a successful career. Such significant circumstances are frighteningly random. We seem to be at the mercy of chance.

Fortunately, this is not important from an NLP viewpoint. Now that we are able to *change* our beliefs, their origin becomes much less significant. In the mean time we simply need to remember that we each start off with a vastly differing portfolio of personal beliefs and values. We are the product of a billion sensual messages from inside and out that carve out our unique neural landscape. And like rain falling on a piece of land, new sensual stimuli tend to follow the path that earlier rains have carved out — the watercourses of the brain we call beliefs. All this explains why George and Bill in the previous chapter reacted so differently to the same message, believed different things about themselves, acted differently, and got different outcomes.

Not all our experience is direct. We read books, watch television, and learn about other environments — other human maps. But all this knowledge reaches the same neural system we used when we were trampled on on the playing field, or embarrassed at a school concert. These second-hand experiences become first-hand when they are recorded in the brain. Sometimes we are not sure whether a 'memory' is real or imagined, or perhaps something we dreamed. At best, our memory is distorted every time we recall and manipulate it. The memories we may actually recall can be memories of memories of memories. So what was never reality in the first place

(being our filtered representation of what happened) becomes less and less real with repeated recall. It is
not surprising that we are able to remember good times
and block out painful memories — and make the good
times seem much better as the years go by. The saying
'time heals' reflects the way we distort memories. The
very process of thinking, as we read a book or listen to
the radio, daydream or fantasise, changes neural patterns
and can form and change beliefs through 'indirect'
experience.

Our beliefs are also affected by the results we have
achieved in the past, our actual performance. If you have
achieved a string of successes it tends to support the
belief that you are good at what you are doing. But if you
have a mixture of results — hits and misses — as most of
us do, you can interpret your behaviour any way you
like. Beginner's luck, however impressive, can soon be
explained away by an experienced veteran, and our
initial inflated self-belief, although based on actual performance, is knocked back to zero. So our beliefs are also
affected by what we have achieved in the past — our
successes and failures if you like, although the terms
'success' and 'failure' are also based on our subjective
perceptions. There is no logic or rationale to this process. A pessimistic person can pull off an impressive
performance and yet interpret his behaviour negatively —
seeing it as a lucky fluke; not expecting to do the same
next time; not believing in himself. Conversely, with a
different attitude, a less 'successful' performer makes
different 'excuses' and goes on to excel, unhampered by
the self-fulfilling prophecy of an unresourceful self-
belief.

We also have beliefs about what has to happen in
order to feel good about an experience. These act as

rules that have to be followed, based on the answer to the question: 'What would have to happen for me to feel loved, free, secure, healthy, or whatever?' In reality, of course, we can feel any of these emotions without specific things 'happening'. But we have given ourselves values or criteria which may unnecessarily and irrationally limit our ability to feel the way we want to feel. These belief-rules ('I have to be a good father,' 'I have to get a better job,' 'I have to get a qualification') may either help or hinder us in getting what we want. A disempowering belief tends to be outside our control, or it is impossible to meet, or it is more likely to make us feel bad rather than good.

NLP approaches belief in a radical way. You can, quite simply, *create* beliefs, and discard old ones. As far as your brain is concerned, you can create experience. It is your choice. You have probably changed your beliefs in the past. Is there anything you believe about yourself today that you did not believe ten years ago? Is there anything you don't believe today that you did then? And what about beliefs about other things, including people, places, or life in general. We are quite able to change our beliefs, and this may well follow a change in environment, circumstances or actual achievements. Neurologically, we just change the way we represent something internally, for whatever reason. We start to use different neural pathways, instead of the old, well-used highways. But this ability we all have to change beliefs is not a tool we consciously use, so we are not in control. We therefore need to identify those beliefs which will empower us, and use the techniques described in this chapter to create them.

EMPOWERING AND DISEMPOWERING BELIEFS

Even small changes at the root level of belief will produce amazing changes in behaviour and performance. This is seen more starkly in children than in adults, as they are more sensitive to suggestion and changing belief. So, for example, if children believe they are good at a sport, or a particular subject, they will *actually* perform better. The better performance will fuel the enhanced self-belief and they will go on to excel.

As we have seen, many leading sportspeople today ascribe their success to an early confidence, a self-belief, often based on the encouragement of a teacher or parent, or the influence of a role model. So-called natural skills, or talents, say in handling numbers, spelling, or playing a musical instrument, cannot be fully explained by genetics, or by education or training. But regardless of their origin, NLP can be used to 'transfer' apparently outstanding skills by gaining an understanding of the mental strategies on which they are based. Those who seem to have special skills from birth *think* in a certain way. Once elicited, their strategy can be learned and used. It is more likely, however, that early 'conditioning' creates and fosters positive self-belief, and the interest, enjoyment of practice, and skill that later appears so natural. Given a strong, positive self-image in a particular area — and we shall learn how to program this — further training and experience will yield far greater results.

In a few rare cases a person might have an overriding self-belief that says 'I'm no good at anything,' and this will have a very damaging effect on anything they try to accomplish — if they even bother to try. But it is far more common to have a mixture of self-beliefs, some of which are positive or 'empowering' and some of which are negative or 'disempowering'. A man might have a very low self-image in career terms and not see himself, for example, as being a good 'manager' or 'boss' or 'leader'. The same person, however, might see himself as a 'natural' at sport, socialising, or in some hobby or pastime. Just as commonly, in a work situation, a woman might rate herself highly in terms of professional ability — being able to do the job well technically — but be far from happy about handling the 'office politics' side of her career. Or vice versa. So we each have a range of self-beliefs, covering the many facets of our work, social and domestic life; and we need to be specific when identifying those that affect what we achieve. We need to replace the disempowering ones with empowering ones.

IDENTIFYING YOUR SELF-BELIEFS

The first step in changing beliefs about yourself is to identify these different facets of how you see yourself — your self-image. You will need to list characteristics or traits that describe you, and what you believe about yourself — not how you think others see you, but how you see yourself. List these in any order, but be ready for a long list, as we have many facets to our personality, and every one has some impact on how we behave and what we achieve. A good technique to get started is to list single words that you feel describe you (like 'honest' or 'untidy'), or double words (like 'self-confident' or 'open-minded') but using your *non-dominant* hand. So, if you are right-handed, use your left hand and vice versa. This may be difficult and you may have to use large block capitals, but it does get easier as you continue. Provided you can interpret each word later, don't be bothered by your childish scribble.

Because your dominant hand, and all that side of your body, is instructed by the opposite side of your brain, you are to some extent harnessing the non-dominant or subconscious side of your two-sided brain. The left side of your brain is concerned with language and logic, and the right side with intuition and feelings. So this simple technique can bring insights from below the conscious level which, although on reflection you know are true, you might not have included on a list done with your usual writing hand. The first semi-legible words you write will probably be predictable and match what you would have listed with your strong hand. As you expand your list, however, allowing your subconscious mind some freedom, you will come up with more revealing self-image words. Where there are apparent contradictions, you need to be honest with yourself as to which one really applies. Often a list written with the dominant hand seems to have been written for 'public consumption', and does not pinpoint deeper self-beliefs. Typically, a dominant hand description 'assertive' might appear as 'blunt', or even 'rude', when described with the non-dominant hand. Usually close friends and relations will confirm that the non-dominant hand description is nearer to the truth. Make out your list, giving yourself all the time you need. It helps if you can relax when doing this. As you reduce the conscious left-brain interference, deeper and franker insights are revealed.

UNDERSTANDING YOUR SELF-BELIEFS

Each of these words can be expanded into one or more specific belief statements. 'Forgetful' might include the specific belief 'I can't remember names' while 'practical' might embrace 'I am good at DIY.' If you are not sure about the exact meaning of some of the words you have written, try to express each one in a sentence — but again using your non-dominant hand. A self-belief can apply to a very specific part of your many-sided personality, and sometimes it is only by calling on the subconscious right side of the brain that you can sort out what you actually believe about yourself. It is these beliefs, revealed by writing them down with the non-dominant hand, then expanded to be more specific, that are likely to account for your behaviour and outcomes, rather than the few you are immediately conscious of.

It is then possible to test each one out in your mind, to confirm whether the submodalities linked to a belief are positive or negative. First, take a positive belief and imagine yourself in an actual situation where your belief is being put into practice. As an example, if you are good at keeping children's attention, say by telling stories, then picture yourself doing it, and enjoying the feeling of doing a good job. This example might have been triggered by the word 'likeable' or 'caring' on your list. To do this you will need to *see* things in your mind — the children's faces, the story book, and anything around you. But to have a more intense experience, you will also need to *hear* any sounds, including your own voice, and also experience any *feelings* associated with what you are doing. In other words, you will have to use your senses, all five if necessary, but especially seeing, hearing and feeling, for the image to become real. As with all these exercises, you should first get into a relaxed, alpha state. You can test out any belief in this way, either by recalling a memory, or by future pacing — visualising some future occasion when you are demonstrating the belief by your actions.

Now switch the scene to something that does not give you pleasure, illustrating a negative self-belief from your list. Let's say, for example, you are giving a formal presentation or speech to some work colleagues. In a thinking sense, *you do not enjoy seeing yourself doing or being this*. Your original word might have been 'reserved', 'shy' or 'private'. Give it a try, either remembering a past experience or imagining a future event, but again make it as real as possible.

So you have experienced two different images of yourself, a positive and a negative one, each reflecting a specific self-belief. If you now compare the submodalities of each scene, you will begin to see differences, not in the content of the two scenarios (that is, telling a children's story as against giving a work presentation), which are obviously very different, but in the nature of the sights, sounds and feelings. These differences are your key to choice and control. For the first time, perhaps, you have been able to understand the structure of your beliefs. Just as you were able to change your feelings, you can utilise your empowering submodalities to create desired beliefs, and change those that are no longer useful. You can identify and use a thinking strategy that gets you results.

Making excuses

As we have seen, our actions are affected by our beliefs, and our beliefs are also affected by our actions, or how we interpret them. In the 1960s some remarkable experiments were carried out involving patients who had had the two sides of their brains surgically separated (usually to reduce the effect of epileptic seizures). This operation involved the severing of the *corpus callosum*, the communication link between the two hemispheres of the upper brain, or cortex. The subjects were shown images on the separate sides of the brain (via the opposite eyes), and asked to point to another image that was related to what they had seen. One subject's left-brain was shown an image of a chicken claw, and his right-brain was shown an image of a snow-covered house. When he was shown a further selection of images and asked to point out images related to what he had just seen, he pointed to pictures of a chicken and a snow shovel, which seemed fine. His reason for choosing the chicken was that he had just seen a chicken claw. However his explanation for choosing the snow shovel was that, 'You need a snow shovel to clean out the chicken shed.' This extraordinary response transformed our understanding of the way we think.

This was not, of course, why he chose the snow shovel, which was obviously related to the snow-covered house. But his right-brain was unable to communicate the image of the snow-covered house to his verbal left-brain. The left-brain, having observed the choice, then *made up a reason!* The verbal left-brain manufactured its own interpretation (in NLP terms its 'excuse') for the action. But the subject did not *know* that he had contrived a relationship — his snow shovel association seemed just as logical to him as the chicken one.

Moreover, the interpretation was made instantly, showing that the brain was adept at giving reasons for any
actions.

Other research has confirmed this remarkable fact,
that people interpret or explain their experiences and
live by those explanations. Normally we do not communicate our excuses to others, at least not in words. We
just store them up and they affect our future behaviour.
Inwardly, we tend to explain our experience in a positive or negative, optimistic or pessimistic way. An
optimistic excuse for missing a three-foot putt in golf
might be, 'That's not like me, it was a fluke' and the
behaviour will be quickly dismissed as insignificant. A
pessimistic excuse for a tennis failure, however, would
go something like: 'Trust me to blow it, my backhand
always lets me down.' A hostess who has served a
delicious meal to special guests might, whatever compli-
ments are flying, form a negative interpretation of the
meal, the whole evening, and any remarks that passed
the lips of her guests. In NLP jargon, she makes *excuses*
about her behaviour. Thus the memory and emotion of
the behaviour is carried over to influence future experience, either positively or negatively, depending on the
excuse.

Notice that the tennis player used the word 'always', which often signals an irrational way of thinking.
Note also that the excuses we give for present behaviour
need not be related to past actual performance. On the
contrary, the hostess might have an enviable record of
cooking and entertaining successes; the pessimistic tennis player might in fact have a better past score than her
optimistic partner. It is just that a positive person tends
to remember the good times, while a negative person
remembers the bad times. So facts are not the issue, but

the *interpretation* of facts, and the state of mind that our interpretation creates which affects what we do. Our individual maps become our reality. And every interpretation of every behaviour enhances that private map of our world.

In the long run, our actual performance will tend to comply with our interpretations, or what we believe about our actions. In the study involving optimists and pessimists referred to at the beginning of the chapter, optimistic insurance salespeople achieved more than 20 per cent higher sales results than their pessimistic colleagues (attitudes like optimism and pessimism are easily assessed in psychometric tests), even though their past experience and training showed no significant difference. In the second year, the optimists outperformed to the extent of 57 per cent, as their positive 'excuses' became self-fulfilling and resulted in even more actual sales. Their optimistic attitude supplied the persistence that any successful salesperson knows is vital, and the state of mind that helps bring about success regardless of interim failures. So what we think about anything — how we interpret it — always affects what we do in the future, and what we achieve. In the end, empowering 'quality excuses' produce quality results.

Learning to be helpless

In 1964 a psychology graduate by the name of Dr Martin Seligman made a remarkable discovery whilst at Princeton University. His fellow students had been doing experiments in which dogs were given mild electric shocks as they tried to find their way out of a maze. Eventually the dogs stopped trying to escape. The more experienced researchers looked for some answer in the dogs, or the way the experiment had been set up, but Seligman, although new to the laboratory, came up with an insight that has had far-reaching effects. He saw that the dogs had *learned* helplessness. Their interpretation of the situation was that it was hopeless to try further, so they stopped trying. Similar experiments were done involving human beings, this time using loud noises. Amazingly, very similar results were obtained — the people stopped trying to escape. They took on the same helplessness. Further experiments then showed that this learned pessimism could be reversed, and once reversed the subjects *never again adopted the helpless state.* So habitual interpretations of our behaviour can be changed, and the new 'excuses' will then form the basis of future behaviour.

Seligman identified specific patterns of belief that caused this feeling of helplessness. The first is permanence. Achievers, when they meet problems, rarely see them as permanent. Secondly, there is pervasiveness. Whilst a problem might be a big one, optimists will not let it affect the rest of their lives so that hopelessness spreads to other areas. The problem is contained, and facts ('I failed, this time') are not translated into untruthful beliefs ('I always fail.') Thirdly, problems and setbacks are not personalised to a 'life level' to become 'I am a failure.' So, without pretending that problems don't exist, we can more accurately describe them in a non-permanent, non-pervasive, non-personal way.

Self-fulfilling spirals

So behaviour does affect belief, first in the interpretation we give to specific actions, and then in gradually creating and reinforcing a self-image. NLP provides ways to intervene in an irrational and otherwise unstoppable downward self-fulfilling spiral, either by intervening in beliefs, or in behaviour, or both.

Most of the things we do every day are done out of habit, with little or no conscious thought. We do other things with more thought and care, and might be ready to give a reason for why we have acted in a particular way, or why we have acted at all. But in all cases what we do, even in minor everyday situations, tends to be governed by what we believe.

Let's take reading a book as an example. What do you do when you read? Some people scribble notes, some use coloured markers, others bend over the corner of the page to show where they are up to. Some people do most of their reading in bed, while others do most on the train to and from work. Some people put a book away, on a shelf perhaps, after each reading session, while others leave the book exactly where they were last reading it, to be picked up — possibly by someone else — after hours, or days. Some people place their books in a logical order on shelves, while others are stored in gay abandon, as likely to be upside down as the right way up.

All these differences in behaviour reflect the differences in you and me, the readers, and, more particularly, our values and beliefs. So a person who does not (as they might describe it) 'deface' a book probably has a *reason* for that behaviour — it is only fair to the next person who might read it, it shows respect for property, it maintains the book's value, and so on. Conversely, another person will probably have reasons for turning over page corners and scribbling notes all over the margins — perhaps to do with creativity, convenience, efficiency, or whatever. So little actions, in themselves innocuous, will tend to fall within a framework of values and beliefs: 'I am a tidy person'; 'I do not waste things'; 'I am organised'; 'I am disorganised'; 'I am thoughtful, clever, punctual, caring, independent. . . .' All these self-images or beliefs are reflected in hundreds of daily, habitual actions. And every action, in turn, by our interpretation of it, reinforces our beliefs and values. We each have a personal hierarchy of excuses covering everything we do, our achievements, failures and general lifestyle.

Every action fits a belief

We are not normally conscious of all this. Only after some thought and analysis will it become apparent that *all* our actions fit into a belief framework. Even a person who prides him or herself on being unpredictable is probably habitually unpredictable, and likely to be a slave to their unpredictable self-image! All this is closely related to the NLP presupposition we met in Chapter 1 which says that behind every action there is a positive intention. There is always some basis for what we do, some purpose, even though it is not immediately apparent to the person behaving — let alone to anyone observing the behaviour.

So our actions are evidence of our beliefs. They are interpreted in terms of belief. And this can work positively or negatively. Using the book example, let us take the action of leaving it wherever you finish reading it, to remain presumably until the next time you want to carry on reading. If the reader has a self-belief which says something like, 'I am a free thinker, I am my own person, I am not a slave to petty rules,' this action will have been *interpreted* (subconsciously) and allocated to that belief. If, however, a strong self-belief says, 'I am untidy,' there is a good chance that this action, along with hundreds of others which may have no other obvious rationale, will find a home in that mental 'I am untidy' pigeon hole, supporting and reinforcing the belief. A little help from an irate partner will no doubt help the untidy self-image along. This is an insidious process whereby otherwise meaningless, trivial actions can make you uncaring, arrogant, slow, forgetful or spiteful — every action will 'fit' some belief. And the stronger these 'disempowering' beliefs become, the more everyday actions are brought into their sinister nets.

BELIEF PIGEON HOLES

There are degrees of action, of course, just as there are degrees of belief. So, as an 'untidy person' self-image ripens and matures, 'book left on the bedroom floor' becomes 'book left on the coffee table or similar', then 'book not returned to shelf', and finally 'book not returned to shelf in the right order'. Just as a child tends to categorise more and more trees as trees, whatever their shape or size as the concept of 'tree' becomes more and more familiar, so we are inclined to deposit more and more of our actions into familiar and convenient belief pigeon holes. Better thinking is not so much to do with preventing this clever filing system, which has its survival advantages, but knowing what the process is and being able to switch between pigeon holes whenever you want to. You can interpret an action in whatever way you want. You can believe whatever you want. Quality thinking requires quality, empowering beliefs.

Spotting your belief pigeon holes

Take some time to check out what we have said so far in your own experience. Make a note of as many of your actions as you can think of throughout a typical day. Now see if you can account for what you do, in terms of your self-beliefs.

For example, you might wash up your coffee mug as soon as you have finished, rather than leaving it until the next coffee break, until it coagulates and grows fungus, or until you run out of crockery. Your reason for this action might be that you don't like an untidy desk (suggesting a belief that 'I am a tidy person'), or you don't want to risk spilling the remains of the coffee (suggesting 'I am careful, considerate, conscientious, respectful of property' etc). Or your reasons might be to do with hygiene, wanting to set an example, or wanting to get away from your desk to socialise. Maybe you are unconsciously fuelling a self-image that says: 'I am a dog's body'; 'I should be in a better job'; 'My talents are wasted'; and so on. This exercise has to be done honestly if it is to be of use.

The number of your actions is more or less unlimited, as are your possible beliefs — even to the level of replacing or not replacing the cap on the toothpaste, a potential cause of marriage breakdown! You will find, however, that a few beliefs keep recurring as pigeon holes for your actions. You might also find that one action (e.g. making an immediate note of any engagement in your diary) supports more than one belief (e.g. 'I am punctual'; 'I am dependable'; 'I am conscientious'; 'I am organised').

As you carry out the exercise you may think of other actions that also support your beliefs. Similarly, you may think of other beliefs or values you did not list earlier but are now aware of because of your actions. Keep any lists or comments you make handy. Finally, try to decide which beliefs are, on balance, *empowering*. These beliefs tend to help you achieve what you want to achieve and be what you want to be. Then try to identify those that are *disempowering*, that tend to stop you reaching your full potential.

You can change those you wish to change using the 'switching submodalities' technique you should now be becoming familiar with. That is, apply the submodalities associated with a behaviour supporting anempowering belief to a behaviour that supports a disempowering belief. Now that you understand the effect of your beliefs on your actions, and can choose whether those beliefs are appropriate, the test of any belief can be: 'Will this belief help me to achieve my outcomes?' The test of your actions will be: 'Is this action congruent with what I believe?'

A JOB WELL DONE

By now you will be becoming familiar with what you do (without thinking) and what you believe (without thinking much about it), and the way they interact. So you are ready for another simple, enjoyable exercise. Think of something you have done well. It is likely to be something that makes you happy when you recall it, just as it gave you pleasure at the time. Don't be modest; we all do some things well. I don't mean we break records every day, or have to compare ourselves with professionals, but to our own standards we are satisfied from time to time with a job well done. If necessary you can use an achievement from the past, but something quite recent is probably better to work on because it is clearer in your mind. Imagine the occasion, or doing what you did, and relive the pleasure it gave you.

Now ask yourself, 'What pleased me about what I did, or how I did it?' and make a note of your answer. Then ask yourself, 'What do I *believe* about myself that my actions — what I did or achieved — are evidence of?' Put the belief into words.

Next, think of three other occasions when you put that same belief into action, different events, actions or achievements that are also evidence of your belief. Try to choose times when other people witnessed what you did, and replay the scenes mentally, as if on a video, from start to finish, in the knowledge that you are living out an important belief. As you do this, say your belief out loud — for example: 'This is a creative, innovative, caring, enthusiastic or whatever, person.' This will strengthen your empowering belief, and also relate it to specific actions — to *evidence of your belief.*

Recall, as vividly as you can, those happy occasions when you did well, living out your belief; then consider how you feel. Doing in your mind what you are good at will bring pleasure and confidence in yourself, and make your belief even more empowering. As you think back to other actions, and identify them with your chosen beliefs, you will be consciously using behaviour to influence belief, which will in turn fuel your confidence to achieve still more. This exercise will *enhance* your already empowering beliefs. You can then, in effect, tune up the submodalities — creating more vivid, associated images — to reflect those associated with your very strongest beliefs, and most motivating experiences.

TURNING ACTIONS INTO EMPOWERING BELIEFS

How can we begin to make every action count towards creating empowering beliefs and achieving our goals? Most of us will readily acknowledge that we are a little short on strong, empowering beliefs — we wish we had greater confidence, were more positive, and could reverse a few negative beliefs. Here is a powerful technique you can try to create any wish you desire. Think of something you would *like* to believe about yourself, but in your heart of hearts you really don't. You might, for instance, want to be open to change and to learning new things, but know that you really find change painful and are slow to take in new knowledge. Think about this, and choose one such belief. Make it something important to you, a belief that could affect a whole range of actions, and ask yourself the following questions.

Is your belief stated positively?

For example, rather than stating a belief such as 'I'm not shy,' which is what you believe you are not, replace it with 'I'm outgoing,' or something similar, expressed positively. Positive statements are more readily accepted by the brain as a sort of subconscious programming.

*Is the belief truly **yours**, and not someone else's?*

For example, 'I believe people like me' is really about somebody else's belief. Restated as 'I'm a likeable person', it becomes more your belief about yourself, and it is now within your control. By acting in a likeable way, although it is inevitable that somebody will not like you,

you can justifiably believe you are a likeable person. The example 'I believe people like me' lacks what I call 'mental credibility' and is not within your power anyway. Express your belief in a form in which you can take full responsibility for proving it by your actions.

Does the belief enhance and respect the rest of your life?

Ask yourself how your chosen belief might affect your goals and plans or, indeed, other values and beliefs you have. You need to be aware of any conflict, any *incongruence* as it is sometimes called, between this belief and other beliefs or goals. An entrepreneur friend strongly believed he could apply himself totally to any task he set himself and succeed, and wanted to enhance his belief and translate it into further achievements. Unfortunately, he had to admit that the belief excluded his wife and family, and in the context of his whole life was not a belief he was happy to see fully enacted. So you may have to amend or change your belief to fit in with the wider ecology of your life and the lives of others that you care about.

Is the belief dynamic or static?

A static belief might be: 'I'm intelligent,' 'I'm reliable' or 'I'm attractive.' The problem with static beliefs is that, as they are expressed absolutely, just one lapse makes them false, and so they lose mental credibility. Now and again, we will all act as though we are far from intelligent, or attractive, or reliable — we just have bad days. We are also subject to comparison — intelligent compared with whom? So inevitably we will come off looking worse than any absolute standard. But a dynamic belief might be: 'I'm becoming more confident,' 'I am becoming a better learner,' 'I am getting better at so and so.' The French psychotherapist, Emile Coue, got it uncannily right almost a century ago when he advised his patients to use the now proverbial formula: 'Every day, and in every way, I am becoming better and better.' A dynamic belief like this remains true, even when we have a temporary relapse. It is *believed* by the subconscious, accepted at face value, and so is readily translated into actual behaviour. This form of positive affirmation allows you the odd 'off day' and, importantly, it allows negative feedback — you get better and better based on what you do wrong rather than what you do right. That is part of true learning.

What actions support the belief?

Now you can take this one stage further. Keeping in mind the belief you want to enhance, think of as many actions as you can that would lead to, or be evidence of, your desired belief. You can think beyond your own experience and imagine others who *do* have such a belief doing the things they do well. What would a person who had this belief actually *do*? Think of as many examples as possible and write them down. For instance, a desired belief, 'I am confident and at ease in any sort of company' will be evidenced in all sorts of ways. Actions might be: making an impromptu speech, making new friends at a social function, hosting an important business lunch, entertaining distant relatives, discussing a sensitive issue with a work colleague, giving a sales presentation to an important client, or helping with a school fete. Try to think of as many actions as you can that are consistent with your desired new belief.

SCREEN PREMIERE

Select an action from the list you have just made and run through it in your mind as if on a movie screen, clearly and in full colour, as realistically as you can. Your visualisation at this stage might involve someone else, if you have no personal success memories to draw upon. But, as soon as you are ready, put yourself into the picture, become the main player, and imagine carrying out the activity personally, with mastery and confidence. See things as if through your own eyes — enter into the experience. Work successively through the sights, sounds and feelings (the modalities that you will by now be familiar with), then bring them all together in a screen premiere. The images are now vivid, you are as good as there, excelling in the activity and enjoying the sensations of pleasure and mastery. While all this is going on, state your belief out loud, affirm it, and let your mind-picture provide all the evidence you need.

You now have a technique you can use, practise and perfect that will create an empowering belief — a belief you *choose* to have. But the process has only just begun. You can visualise other actions from your list that will reinforce your belief. Your aim is to become familiar with all sorts of actions (for the moment represented by the electrochemical changes in your brain as you imagine) that give evidence of your belief. Each activity supporting your single, desired belief should be played out in your imagination. So many outstanding achievers account for their success in this way. You can then move on to other desired empowering beliefs using the same process.

COMMIT YOURSELF

One stage remains, and this is likely to get the adrenaline pumping. Decide where and when you are going to put your visualised actions into practice — at home, socially, at work, wherever an opportunity might arise in the near future. Get out your diary and start making commitments. If you are involved in a regular work meeting, this might be a chance to try some new assertiveness techniques, or you might know of an opportunity coming up to give a public speech or presentation. Arrange to start a new pastime, sport or activity. Your list should be long enough to suggest at least a few actions that you can schedule into your real life. Commit yourself. Tell people what you have decided to do. If you get a bit nervous, that's fine. Keep up your visualising, as this will build up your confidence for the real thing. Do your homework. Learn what you need to learn and make any necessary preparations. It will all be worthwhile because you are about to change not just major areas of behaviour but the fundamental self-beliefs on which they are based; beliefs that will change you for the better and for good.

These exercises can be applied to each of your desired empowering beliefs in turn. Then you can transfer your new-found mastery from one application to another, say from a sport to a hobby to a career matter, creating a balance between work, social and more personal areas of your life. You are learning how to make every action count. You now know what to do to have the greatest impact on your beliefs, and the greatest chance of fulfilling your goals. Based on the few principles we outlined in the first chapter, and simple neurological facts about the way your brain operates, you are acquiring the skills to make very profound personal changes, and get whatever you want.

5
Dreaming Your Way to Success

▼

WHAT YOU DREAM ABOUT, or imagine, will have an effect on what actually happens in your life. It seems that we are born with the ability to make mental maps of reality before living out those maps. We first imagine what we want to happen, or what we would like to be, and thus 'experience' our reality internally before embarking on it in the external world. That experience will embrace all the sights, sounds and feelings that we associate with the real thing, along with the feeling of pleasure it brings — or, in the case of something we worry about (a negative use of the imagination), the feeling of pain.

THE IMPORTANCE OF IMAGINATION

Albert Einstein wrote that, 'Imagination is more important than knowledge.' His theory of relativity equation $E = mc^2$ started as a crazy, imaginative cosmic journey on a ray of light. Many other scientific breakthroughs, although accompanied — as was Einstein's — by much hard work and perseverance, can also be traced to some imaginative leap. It seems that goal-achievers, or high performers, are able to imagine, or mentally rehearse, their achievements, sometimes long before they come to fruition. Athletes will often practise success first in their minds, before an actual performance, sometimes basing their visualisation on a role model better than themselves. And experiments have proved that performance does, in fact, improve as a result of mental practice, just as with physical practice. In the case of throwing darts and basketball free throws, for example, researchers were amazed to find that so-called mental rehearsal was just about as effective as actual, physical practice. And similar results have been shown in selling and other business applications, all confirming the importance of the imagination in actual achievement.

Imagination is a universal, natural ability, and we use it all the time. If we repeatedly imagine the worst about a forthcoming event or experience, this will tend to affect what actually happens, because we are programming our behaviour by the way we think. Similarly, if we enjoy a certain sport or pastime, we tend to practise and enjoy it mentally. The repeated 'success recordings' then give us the confidence to perform better in reality. In most cases this process seems to work by accident or default. Although each of us may excel in a handful of activities, we have not been able to recognise and transfer whatever we are doing right mentally from one situation to another. So we might have a low self-image in one area and a high self-image in another, neither having any rational basis. Having recognised the important part that imagination plays in anything we do, NLP allows us to start using it consciously and constructively, to enhance our performance in any area we choose.

WISHES AND WANTS

We are all a product of our dreams. Your house, your car, the places you have been to, were once just imaginings — personal maps of reality. The books on your shelves were once someone else's dreams, as was your local shopping centre. Somebody imagined the chair you are sitting on before it became a design on paper, then a reality. That is how things happen. So, to get what you want, you first need to harness the power of your imagination. The quality of your dreams determines the quality of your life, so it pays to be choosy about what you imagine. Always go for the best.

Some 'dreams' never become reality. They remain just wishes. As mental imagery, they are of poor quality, and not much use in producing top performance. But we can apply NLP techniques to upgrade wishes into wants, and half-baked fancies into powerful, motivating desires. We can learn to create quality dreams.

Changing wishes into wants

Try this little exercise. Think of one or two wishes — things that you would like to happen but in your heart of hearts you don't rate the chances very highly. Now picture each wish being fulfilled, seeing yourself and the surrounding circumstances as you imagine they would be if the wish were to come true. As you imagine the sights, sounds and feelings, you will probably find they are distant, vague or blurred — in other words not like the real thing. It is probably difficult to dwell on the image for more than a few moments. This is how a wish, or 'poorly formed outcome', is represented in your mind.

Now switch your thoughts to a strong desire or want, which you really believe will come about, something that, although it has not yet actually happened, you can vividly imagine and enjoy. The sights, sounds and feelings associated with this desire are likely to be close and clear, and easy to visualise. Within a few minutes you will be able to experience, not just each of the inner senses or modalities, but the feelings of pleasure. So, in a technical, thinking sense, you can have a wish or a want; a good-quality dream or a bad-quality dream; a well-formed outcome or a poorly formed outcome. Each is represented very differently neurologically. More importantly, it is the clear, vivid, good-quality dream that will tend to happen. Because we can develop our ability to imagine, both generally and in each modality, and can also change specific submodalities (like making a picture bigger and brighter), we can influence both the chances of the outcome happening, and also the quality, or level of achievement, of the outcome itself.

YOUR AUTOMATIC GOAL-ACHIEVING SYSTEM

As human beings we seem to be drawn towards clearly imagined goals. They represent the target in a cybernetic system like the ones used in missiles, industrial robots or a domestic central heating system Most life-goals, such as breathing and other body functions, are 'pre-wired'. We constantly achieve the right body temperature and pulse rate — just as a heating system maintains the temperature in a room. But the system also works for higher level goals that we can consciously 'input' to the system, including the goals you listed in Chapter 2. Our senses provide the necessary feedback, constantly monitoring where we are in relation to our goal, and all our physical and mental powers provide the 'propulsion' to amend our actions until they exactly mirror the internal goal. If something does not work, we try something else, and errors — like over-steering when learning to drive a car — are progressively reduced as we move nearer the target of a desired skill or achievement. During this cybernetic or steering process, useful ideas might come, apparently from nowhere, but these are triggered by association with an existing goal. Provided the target is clear we will move relentlessly towards it. Fortunately this is an unconscious learning process — the unconscious competence we discussed in Chapter 1. So all we need to be concerned about is fixing and maintaining a clear goal — programming our brain to do what we could never accomplish consciously.

APPLYING THE POWER OF THE IMAGINATION TO YOUR GOALS

When you worked out your list of goals in Chapter 2, each of the tests you used to clarify them simply applied common sense and logic. You did not apply any tests of imagination but you did have to formulate each goal clearly. If you were not easily able to describe a particular goal in words, this could indicate that it falls into the 'wish' category. As well as being hard to describe, it will also be hard to visualise. Similarly, if there are problems of ecology — the goal generates some conflict, or there are feelings of uneasiness — this might suggest a desire about which you have not sorted out your priorities. Here again, it is unlikely that you will be able to visualise a clear, realistic image of the outcome happening. But now, based on the way you learnt to differentiate between a wish and a want, you can start to rank your list of goals according to how clearly you can imagine them; how well they are etched internally — on the hard disk of your mind and imagination. You may need to go back to the checklist of submodalities on page 66/7 to remind yourself how to analyse each visualised goal.

Enhancing your imagined goals

If you want to skip the process of comparing the characteristics of all your goals, and get on with achieving actual changes, there is a short cut. Simply choose your three top goals, and imagine them clearly. Make the images big, colourful and focused, the sounds loud and clear, and all the feelings as real as life. If you are part of the picture, see and experience everything as through your own eyes, not as an outsider. Experience each modality — seeing, hearing and feeling — and 'enhance' all the imagery to make it lifelike. Then dwell for a while on the overall feeling this brings, and enjoy it. Do this from time to time so that it becomes easy to get into the visualised outcome quickly, and the images become more and more realistic. You are now creating good-quality dreams, establishing cybernetic targets, and starting a process which will turn your subjective thoughts into objective reality. You have learned to dream constructively, to fulfil your own purposes.

Changing weak goals into strong goals

If you are ready to work through all your listed goals, you can go a stage further. You can start to identify the submodalities that represent your strongest desires, and those you associate with the greatest pleasure. And it is these submodalities, or personal thinking characteristics, that you should then apply to the weaker goals and wishes. If, for example, your strongest desires seem to be larger than life, rather than lifesize, this is how you should represent your other less-focused goals to get maximum effect. So if an image is small and distant, deliberately make it larger than life. Similarly, if you visualise a panoramic scene in your strongest images, rather than a framed screen, then use this submodality throughout.

For *you*, the panoramic image means effective thinking and success — you have a winning model. In this exercise you are exploring your own personal, subjective world. You are learning how successful thinking strategies are formed for you. You can continue to learn from what works best, building success on success.

You may want to discuss this with a relative or friend as you go along. You might be surprised at what you learn about how other people 'think'.

GOALS OR DREAMS?

The list of goals you decided upon earlier might not be the same as your 'dreams'. You may have downgraded a goal you thought was not feasible, or amended it in some way, based on the checklist. Goals are not exactly dreams. They are just desires with a deadline, or milestones on the way towards dreams. A dream always exceeds a well-specified, articulated goal. And as you achieve one goal, you will have already formed a dream of something bigger and better. The goal planning you did in Chapter 2 is mostly a logical, left-brain activity. The imagining in this chapter is a right-brain activity. Using both sides of your brain results in holistic, powerful thinking, the sort that stimulates actual behaviour. So don't let logic and the cold light of reason restrict your dreams. The means will only be found if the dream is strong enough to drive you forward. Insurmountable obstacles only become surmountable if you *believe* you will reach your dream; and this belief is represented by a clearly imagined dream fulfilled. Even so-called willpower has to be channelled in a direction — the direction of a clear goal, an indelible dream.

Mental imagery offers a pattern for improvement in any walk of life, and several NLP techniques have been developed for particular applications. Let us say, for example, that your dream is to excel in some sport or activity requiring special skill, talent or perhaps charisma, as might be the case with public speaking or entertaining. First, picture yourself (dissociated, that is watching from outside) doing the particular activity, with all the flair and skill you can imagine. Next, become yourself (associated, that is seeing everything through your own eyes) and again experience the feeling of excellence as you perform with whatever skills you need in your imagination. If you have difficulty with the transition from a dissociated image to an associated one (seeing through your own eyes), try imagining that a mist clouds the first scene. When it clears you are in the new, associated mode — look down and see your own hands and feet.

Next think of someone who you can easily imagine doing just what you dream of being able to do. It could be a top professional you have seen on television, or perhaps a friend or colleague you envy. It doesn't matter. Just clearly imagine them, rather than yourself, excelling in the activity, and watch exactly what they do. Is there anything about their performance you want to incorporate into yours? Is there any way you can improve? How do you think they feel? Can you imagine that, too? Now let a mist envelop the image of the model performer. As the mist clears, become yourself again, making any changes you wish to make having observed your model, feeling how you want to feel, and honing the performance to whatever level of excellence you can imagine. Then savour the pleasure of the experience for a while. You have now formed a quality dream, drawing on the best models your imagination cares to use. With practice, this should compare in its clarity and realness with your visualisation of any other activity at which you are skilled and super-confident.

MAKE A DATE

Now back to your left-brain, and some practicalities. Decide when you will next be able to do the activity you have imagined, write it in your diary, and commit yourself. If it's golf, get yourself fixed up with an appropriate partner. If it's chairing a meeting at work, decide on the next chance you will have to display your imagined performance. If it's cooking, plan the occasion that will allow you to exhibit your skill. If at all possible, commit yourself to more than one occasion — *create* opportunities to turn your dreams into reality. This commitment is important, as it is likely that an area of under-performance has been subject to a negative self-image. You will therefore tend to make ingenious excuses and find reasons why you cannot have a go at what you want to do. Then keep up the visualisation. This is an ongoing process and not a one-off miracle cure for all your deficiencies. And don't give up on anything else that common sense tells you is needed, like keeping fit, dieting, hard work, perseverance, reading books — even though these have not worked in the past. Be confident that all your efforts will be more effective now that your unconscious autopilot has been 'programmed' with good-quality dreams.

When it comes to getting what you want, NLP can convert a wish into a want, a general interest into a powerful passion. This brings with it a new confidence in yourself and your ability to achieve any goal you seriously set for yourself. Even a negative emotion like envy can be harnessed to bring about the fulfilment of your own purposes — if someone is good enough to envy they are a useful model for NLP mastery techniques. You don't have to be a naturally ambitious, goal-oriented person to start achieving great things. You can start with fickle wishes and ill-formed desires, but learn to apply better thinking to them — learn to make better dreams. And if you are a natural goal-setting planner, at home with tasks, resolutions and 'to-do' lists, you can complement that logical, sensible approach in a natural and enjoyable way, adding important, right-brain skills — skills that will make the all-important difference to what you actually achieve. Don't worry; these skills will not make you a *dreamer* (dreamers don't produce worthwhile results because they don't know how to translate dreams into reality). But, if you are to achieve something worthwhile, you *do* have to have a dream.

6

Your Inner Team

▼

YOU ARE PROBABLY FAMILIAR with an inner voice, or feeling, that takes part in most aspects of your life. Sometimes the voice can be a friend, encouraging you to have a go, but all too often it is critical, casting doubts on your abilities, and running counter to your natural instincts which say 'I can do it.' Part of you might take an instant like or dislike to a person you meet, but without consciously knowing why. Sometimes we refer to this sort of reaction as 'chemistry', a 'gut feeling', or maybe a 'hunch'. As we learned in Chapter 4 we often have conflicting beliefs based on all sorts of internal and external influences, and even our main self-beliefs can sometimes work against each other. So when we try to achieve our goals, we are bombarded by other parts of ourselves; an inner, well-meaning 'team' that can help or hinder what we are trying to do.

MULTIPLE PERSONALITIES

When you did the non-dominant hand self-belief exercise in Chapter 4, you probably wrote some one- or two-word descriptions of yourself which were contradictory, almost as though different people were expressing themselves through the conscious and non-conscious parts of your brain. Hundreds of delegates at my seminars have been amazed at what they have written about themselves using this simple technique. For example, the dominant hand's 'outgoing' can easily become the non-dominant hand's 'arrogant', and 'reserved' can become 'withdrawn' in the franker words that the childlike right-brain chooses. But often descriptions on the non-dominant list seem to directly contradict those on the dominant list. For instance, you might get 'outgoing' contrasted with 'private', or 'organised' as opposed to 'carefree'.

These different descriptions, apparently contradictory, represent different facets of how we see ourselves. On further amplification into sentences (using the same non-dominant hand technique) it usually transpires that we are describing ourselves in different situations or at different times, or even using images from the past which still affect us. For instance, one word might reveal a self-image in a work context, while we might take on a different view of ourselves at home or socially. We might call ourselves artistic, which at times we are, but also see ourselves as practical, which is also a part of us. This technique reveals the many different ways in which we see ourselves, and also reflects the different personalities inside which can vie for expression from time to time.

The very idea of multiple personalities would have been ridiculed not long ago, but now all the evidence points to different 'minds' at work in each of us. The split-brain research of Roger Sperry established what was termed the *two mind theory*, which is now confirmed by our knowledge of the entirely different ways the left and right sides of the brain operate. So, while the language-based left-brain will account for different self-beliefs about how we are organised, communicate, solve problems, make decisions and criticise, the holistic right-brain reveals all kinds of self-beliefs concerned with creativity, expression, relationships and how we feel. Some of these aspects of how we think, feel and believe are so distinct that they take on the characteristics of an inner team of different personalities. To different degrees they are part of everything we think, say, do and achieve.

Each of us can probably recall times when we have been highly organised, logical and in control, and other times when we have been as carefree, instinctive and disorganised as little children. Although this 'team' can sometimes seem to be out of control, creating all sorts of conflicts that prevent us from pursuing our goals single-mindedly, all these aspects of ourselves are, in truth, allies. They mean well! Some part of us is being expressed in every action, even when it is in apparent conflict with other parts of us, and not consciously understood. ('Behind all behaviour is a positive intention' is the presupposition we met in Chapter 1.) We also came across this concept when setting clear goals in Chapter 2 in what was called the *ecology check*. You probably found that some of your goals conflicted with others, as though one was fulfilling the desire of one person inside, and another a different person. One goal might have been to do with security, while another might have involved change and uncertainty. These have to be reconciled if your actions are to be congruent and goal-directed. By thinking through the possible implications of each goal and working out compromises or modifications, you can take these ecology factors into account. We shall now try to understand this inner 'team' better so that we do not just negatively make allowances for them by compromise, but can start positively using them as our personal inner resource.

YOUR INNER CRITIC

Timothy Gallwey, a top British tennis player and coach, wrote the successful book *The Inner Game of Tennis*, and later *The Inner Game of Golf*. His coaching methods have been very effective in both games and are significant in NLP terms because of his understanding of the mental processes involved. He was not satisfied with the progress of his tennis students, who seemed unable to cope with a stream of helpful corrective advice. Then, almost by accident, he discovered that if they simply watched him do a stroke a few times and copied it, with no instruction or criticism, they did better than with conventional detailed instruction. And this applied to novices as well as experienced players. It seemed that if players were thinking, consciously, of what they were doing, they performed worse than if they were not 'thinking', but just *doing*, or copying, as a child might learn any new game. So he reduced his instruction to an absolute minimum and his results improved.

He discovered that we each have an inner equivalent of an instructor, or critic, who constantly tells us what we should be doing. 'Watch your feet,' 'Slow down a little,' 'Faster now,' 'Watch the ball,' 'Mind your breathing.' And this inner critic, just as much as any external critic, adversely affects performance. Gallwey identified two 'selves' at work. Self 1 was the knowledgeable, well-meaning but judgemental critic who always interfered, and Self 2 was the natural tennis-player who, left alone, could play the game with natural, instinctive talent. Self 1 thought he was the expert, but he wasn't. Self 2 was a confident, natural player who enjoyed the game, but was hampered and bullied by his wise, articulate Self 1. By using techniques to distract Self 1, in order to let Self 2 get on with playing, Gallwey was able to produce outstanding results. He then went on to introduce similar mental techniques into the game of golf, proving their potency through his own rapid rise in the game from novice level.

The two selves that Gallwey discovered (with no experience of the working of the brain and the important findings of recent years) were, of course, the same distinct 'minds' that Nobel prizewinner Roger Sperry discovered in his work with split-brain patients. The critical Self 1 is the logical, articulate left-brain, while the natural, expressive, childlike, inarticulate Self 2 corresponds to the right-brain.

But this inner critic is not just present in sports. Often our own 'self-talk' bombards us with criticism in all sorts of situations: 'You'll never do that,' 'Be careful,' 'What will so-and-so think?' 'Have you thought about . . .?' Sometimes this inner dialogue is supportive ('Go on, you can do it' or 'I'll show them') and empowers us in what we are doing. Most of the time, however, negative self-beliefs block our true potential. If asked to give an immediate impromptu speech we often perform far better than if we have been given plenty of notice. In the latter case our inner critic has plenty of time to advise, warn and interfere and the other self is bombarded into mute terror. You will remember the learning model we met in the Chapter 1, in which we excel when we are unconsciously competent. In Self 2 mode we are not thinking in a conscious sense, and the critic is not at work. So, while driving your car the left-brain can be attending to a radio programme, deciding what to cook for dinner, or working out how to face an angry client. While Self 1 is so distracted, Self 2 drives from A to B with 'unconscious competence'.

A business colleague had hurt his leg but, out of courtesy, agreed to play a prearranged round of golf with a friend. He was in a lot of pain, and could think of nothing but his leg all through the game; he was looking forward to getting it over with and returning home to rest. But, to his astonishment, he finished the game with his highest score ever! By not 'thinking' about the game, because his mind was preoccupied with his injured leg, he was able to perform at his best. Although we cannot always manipulate such circumstances, Timothy Gallwey uses the principle of diverting the attention of the conscious mind very effectively. Other athletes, public speakers and entertainers have developed their own techniques to allow right-brain mastery to overcome critical, self-conscious, left-brain thinking. This includes correct breathing and relaxation (which can remove the 'busy' thoughts associated with the left-brain) and specific visualisation, or the NLP future pacing techniques that we have already met.

GETTING TO KNOW YOUR INNER TEAM

You are probably familiar with the inner critic that Gallwey identified, as it is very much part of your conscious, left-brain thinking. We have many parts to us, but some of these are far from familiar, operating unconsciously as they do. Each of these parts, however, has an effect on our behaviour. When we are confronted with behaviour that has no rational explanation, whether in others or in ourselves, we are confronting some part that is not operating visibly and consciously.

For example, whilst we can easily imagine a part of us wanting to get rid of back pain, we do not as easily identify a part of us that wants to keep the pain — perhaps because of the extra care and attention we receive, as a topic of much needed conversation in a relationship, a reason not to start some new strenuous task, an excuse for turning down invitations to social events, a reason for claiming the best chair, for not carrying out the weekly rubbish bag, for not getting up to put the kettle on, or whatever. Each of the above secondary benefits, or outcomes, will militate, unconsciously but very effectively, against the conscious outcome 'I want to get rid of my back pain.' These intentions might be misguided, irrational or stupid. But the point is that they are viewed positively, as being beneficial or pleasurable, by some part of us. Our natural desire for pleasure and the avoidance of pain then creates a 'conflict' in which we cannot stop ourselves from doing what we (consciously) do not want to do.

These conflicts show up in many ways, not just as unwanted habits and behaviour patterns, but in the way we react to events, situations, tasks, people, and all manner of day-to-day stimuli. The back pain illustration applies just as well to smoking, drinking and other drug abuse, overeating, anger, resentment and any behaviour that might not be rationally chosen or explained but in which some secondary benefit is likely to be present. Not surprisingly, it is the actions we do not consciously control that have the biggest influence over achievements — the others are taken care of. In order to make changes, we have to be ready to identify those parts of us that motivate unwanted, disempowering behaviour.

Doing an exhaustive non-dominant hand list of self-descriptions will take you a long way towards identifying these hidden parts of you. You can probably relate them to specific situations, or to specific unwanted habits. What we usually finish up with is *many* parts, or selves. We are complex, multifaceted individuals, with a bewildering personal hierarchy of beliefs, attitudes, feelings, desires and intentions, all of which reveal themselves, in some way, in what we do.

There are NLP techniques to help us identify these parts, and to unify those which are in conflict. As we are, by definition, involving our subjective minds, the right side of the brain, techniques that use all the modalities of imagination, rather than just cold, verbal logic, are more effective. So you will have to be ready to switch to 'pretend' mode from time to time, and not stay within the limitations of rational thought.

The inner team party

The following is a general technique for identifying and communicating with parts of yourself. This is typical of several NLP approaches and you can adapt it as you wish.

1. Relax and get into alpha and imagine a pleasant, comfortable place somewhere outside (perhaps in a sunny meadow). Create a table with six chairs round it.

2. Ask your unconscious mind to think of two parts

of yourself that you are **really happy with**, and let them take their place as guests at the table. Let these come from your subconscious — whichever two come to your mind first. Welcome your guests.

3. Then ask your unconscious mind for two parts of your mind that you find **useful and practical**, and welcome these also to your table, thanking them for taking part.

4. Next ask your unconscious mind for two parts of yourself that you particularly **dislike** and with which you are unhappy. Be equally courteous in welcoming these also. Then have all your six guests introduce themselves and become acquainted.

5. Ask your guests: 'Who here feels the most misunderstood?' Ask the one who responds: 'Please let us know what your positive purpose is — what special benefit you want to bring to me.' Listen to the answer and write it down if you wish. Make sure that the others have understood and appreciated the importance of what this member of the team is trying to do for you.

6. Ask the same question of the other five: 'Who among the rest of you feels the most misunderstood?' Then ask the question of the one who responds: 'What is your positive intention, the benefit you want to bring to me?' Listen for the answer, and again be sure that the others understand and appreciate what has been said.

7. Repeat this process for the remaining four, then three parts.

8. When there are two parts remaining who have not contributed, ask them both also to say, one at a time, what positive benefits they bring to the table, and notice again that everyone round the table understands the different contribution that each part is bringing.

9. Watch as the table fades away, all six members of your team hold hands, and you stand in the centre, enjoying the different gifts and benefits that each has brought to you. Slowly come back to your objective world and notice how you feel.

This party idea is just a metaphor that can unlock some right-brain secrets. You can change it to some other scenario if you wish, but stick to the principles of the technique. Notice the importance of getting agreement at each stage of the process, making the different parts aware of each other's contributions. How you personify, symbolise or otherwise represent an inner part is entirely up to you. If each one takes on a personality of its own, communication becomes much easier than if you try to deal with abstractions.

This exercise calls on highly subjective, right-brain skills, and there are simple devices to help the imaginative process along. If you cannot visualise a part of yourself, imagine what the part might look like if you could — *pretend* that you can!. The purpose of the exercise is not to get a 'correct' image or representation, but any representation that helps you to communicate. Similarly, if you cannot imagine a response, try to imagine what they might say if you could. All these 'what if' devices are legitimate in subjective exploration. What seems contrived and unnatural will soon become second nature as you get more in touch with yourself, and trust your ability to communicate inwardly as well as outwardly.

This can be a very empowering and motivating technique, as you become aware, perhaps for the first time, of the support of your inner team. You will start to look on the 'less desirable' parts of yourself in a different light. You should begin to feel, in a very literal sense, more at one with yourself.

USING YOUR INNER TEAM

If you feel happy with this technique, you may wish to try to identify inner parts more specifically. In this case you should think of a specific behaviour or habit that you would like to change — something you can see no benefit in and would rather do without. Get into alpha and try to get in touch with those parts of you that are trying to bring about their positive purposes for you through your actions. There may be one or more parts involved. One part might generate the behaviour, and other parts might have objections (as you do at a conscious level). You can use the same outdoor party metaphor or, now you are familiar with the process, any other scenario you care to invent.

Using the technique in the way described might identify some intentions that you were not aware of, as in the bad back example. Once these conflicting purposes are brought to a conscious level, you can start making choices, rather than remaining at the mercy of habitual behaviour for which you have no rational explanation. In the light of what you learn, you may decide to carry on doing what you are doing even though your behaviour is not ideal. Alternatively, you might think of better ways to achieve the outcomes that your unacceptable behaviour is trying to achieve. Try to identify different parts of yourself by using different examples of undesirable behaviour, attitudes and beliefs.

Once we know how different parts of us think, we can solve problems of all kinds and achieve challenging outcomes. Most complex problems and goals require several different ways of thinking. For instance, although there might be a creative stage in what we are doing, we may also need to be highly organised, and able to plan on a more pragmatic, conscious level. The inner critic that Timothy Gallwey spotted in his tennis students can be a useful ally in some circumstances. How many husbands and wives have been grateful for the restraining influence of their partner when they might have done something foolhardy without some firm, objective criticism? And our own critical self-talk, although it might stunt raw creativity, will usually keep our feet firmly on the ground and ensure we have not overlooked important factors. So it is important to recognise the different roles of our inner parts in bringing about an overall outcome that none of them, alone, could successfully achieve.

Imagine you want to make some major changes to your garden, but within a limited budget and timescale. First you need creativity and the ability to visualise what you have in mind. Then you need a lot of organising ability to bring together the many parts of the project within the constraints of time and money. But you also need to be self-critical at each stage, act as devil's advocate from time to time, and foresee any problems before it is too late to remedy them. All three parts have a role to play, but none can act successfully in isolation. The problem is that these useful parts, which we all have in some measure, often work against each other rather than together. So the creative part gets annoyed at the restrictions imposed by the organiser, the organiser cannot cope with the uncertainty of the creative ideas, and the critic, who constantly irritates both these parts, cannot understand how they could both overlook the obvious. All this conflict stops you making decisions and getting things done, even though you have more than enough thinking power to cope.

Your problem-solving trio

There is a technique that brings together these three parts. But first you need to check that all three are represented in you. Think of a time when you have been truly creative. Maybe this is not the way you see yourself all the time, but now and again we all come up with really inspired, effective ideas. Think of such a time, and experience all the modalities clearly. Notice how it feels to be such a creative person. For the following exercise, this is your creative self. Now think of a time when you did a great organising job. It might have been to do with setting up a new office system, moving house, arranging a wedding, planning a holiday or whatever, but you had it all under control. This is you operating with mastery as a practical organiser. And finally, imagine yourself as a critic, being cautious but wise and far-seeing as you brought common sense and reality into some situation. Recall yourself in this role, maybe as a parent, boss or other authority figure. Having gone through each visualisation vividly, you should be familiar with what it feels like to take on each role. While you were doing this your physiology probably changed, too. Try going from one state to another, becoming each self in turn, and experiencing the feelings associated with each one.

Now you are prepared to solve problems with your new-found allies — your inner team. Think of a current problem, one which you have not been able to overcome to date, so the exercise will be of real value.

1. Relax into alpha, get into your **creative** mode and think of any ideas you can that address your problem. Don't worry about whether the ideas will work, or if they seem far-fetched — just generate some good ideas.

2. Now get into your **practical, organising** mode. It sometimes helps if you physically move to a different position, or you might not fully switch modes. In any case you should break your state in some physical way. Recite a quick nursery rhyme, do a jig, or something. In your practical, organising state, you will feel super-efficient, as you did earlier. In this role you should think of everything that has to be done to put the creative ideas into operation: things you have to prepare and plan for; information you have to get; people you have to involve. Try to think of everything, using the same mental power you used when you actually performed in such a way.

3. When you have tied up any loose ends and know just what has to be done, change state as you did before and become your **critical** self. You may want to sit on an upright chair, taking on the role of a judge. Now think of anything that might go wrong and reasons why the ideas, and your strategies for making them happen, might founder. Don't pull any punches. Be as critical as you like.

4. You are probably left with some ideas that sounded good until you considered their practical implications, and some practical solutions which sounded fine until the inner critic got to work. Now start the cycle again. Get back to your **creative** state and think of creative ways to counter the criticisms and objections. Be just as creative as you were at the beginning, but this time address only the remaining objections. Expect to receive plenty of ideas.

5. Once again change state to become the **organiser**. Now, in your resourceful, super-efficient state of mind, say what actually needs to be done to implement these last ideas.

6. Then once again, give your **critic** the chance to come up with objections. These objections will probably be fewer, and more specific, than on the previous occasion.

7. Go back to your **creative** state and come up with more ideas that address these remaining objections — and so on, until the last objection has been overcome, and you have an idea that is practical, and which has stood the test of criticism.

Using your inner mastery in these areas, as a team, you have done what each part would not have accomplished alone. (Normally, a winning idea can be quickly silenced by your critic, who will not agree to continue the search for a solution, labelling the whole idea as 'impossible'.) This is a powerful technique for harnessing existing, natural thinking skills.

Thinking hats

Edward de Bono, of lateral thinking fame, uses a variation of the inner parts idea as a general communication tool for all sorts of situations, including business meetings and negotiations. He uses the metaphor of thinking hats, using six different-coloured hats to denote different ways of thinking. The **white** hat is neutral and objective, just concerned with objective facts and figures. The **red** hat expresses emotions, giving an intuitive point of view. A **black** hat denotes a negative perspective (in effect showing why something can **not** be done), and a **yellow** hat a positive, optimistic viewpoint. A **green** hat is a metaphor for the creative self you have just been using. And finally, a blue hat is concerned with controlling and organising the whole thinking process; how to best marshal all the different ways of thinking. By metaphorically wearing each hat you take on that particular way of thinking, as you did in the last exercise. And this can be made known, in a meeting or group situation — 'Wearing my yellow hat, I think we are on to a winner' — so that the difference in thinking mode is allowed for. By using the hat metaphor, for instance, it is acceptable to give an intuitive rather than objective view, or suggest a negative aspect even though you are personally optimistic. Contributions are thus elicited that would otherwise have remained unspoken, and the usual emotional and personal blockages are avoided.

This method can be used in any team setting, where different thinking approaches are needed to arrive at a decision. It can also be used as a metaphorical checklist to expand your personal thinking and the quality of your decisions. When required, *everyone* can wear a creative hat, or take an optimistic or pessimistic view to get both perspectives, or offer an intuitive input without the need to justify it logically. In this way, just as in the 'team party' technique, each way of thinking has its contribution acknowledged, and no single mindset (fixed direction of thought), whether logical or intuitive, positive or negative, creative or practical, predominates. By metaphorically changing hats, it is acceptable to think in a different way, where it might otherwise not have been considered sufficiently 'macho' or objective. De Bono's method operates at a far more general, stereotypical level than many NLP techniques which address our thinking at an unconscious level. But you might find this simpler method useful if you have difficulty in identifying and getting responses from specific parts of you, or in a group setting.

Here is an example of how the hat method could help solve a personal problem. Paul and Janice have been married for about ten years. They have no children, would both like to have a child, and are both currently working. Janice feels that a mother's place is with the child at home, at least for the first two years. Giving up her job to have the baby they want would more or less halve their income and they are afraid of the financial strains they would face.

The couple first wear their **white** hats and simply list the facts: married for ten years; want baby; Janice prefers to be with baby, etc. Then, with their **red** hats on, they express their feelings, regardless of pros and cons, or logic. Paul might say how depressed he gets because of not being able to provide fully for a family; he might have doubts about being a father, or not being so important in Janice's life if a baby came along; or he may have doubts about a major change in lifestyle. Janice might be jealous of friends who are far better off; she might be scared about a drop in standard of living after so long; or she might feel guilty that she is putting material things before the baby. She may be angry that her career has to be interrupted rather than Paul's.

Putting on their **black** hats, they think of all the negatives: 'Why change a happy, dependable relationship?' 'Halving our income, with increased costs, we'll never recover financially.' 'Who wants to bring up a child in this day and age in any case?' 'You'll lose your career chances if you don't get back to work within six months of having a baby.' Janice is sure she'll never lose weight after being pregnant. Then the **yellow** hat — thinking of all the positive things: 'A baby will make the family complete.' 'He or she will provide for us in our old age.' 'Think of the joy it will bring to our parents.' 'I could take a second job if necessary — it's worth it.' The **green** hat is for creativity: things that Janice can do from home to earn extra money; or childcare work so she can take the baby with her; part-time work for Paul; ideas for economising on living costs; starting the business they have both talked about before — taking the risk.

Now they bring it all together, wearing their **blue** hats. Is this sort of decision better based on intuition or logic? They compare the optimistic and pessimistic ideas, and weigh them up. There might be more facts they need to get together before a final decision is made. They might need another **green** hat brainstorming session to solve one aspect of the decision that seems to bother them more than others. In this way a sound decision is almost sure to emerge, based on appropriate thinking, and involving both parties to the full.

By subjecting otherwise intractable problems to these techniques you will be amazed at how solutions emerge. Sometimes a problem seems to disappear even before the technique is completed, as new viewpoints are identified. And even if no specific solution is forthcoming, a problem can be changed out of all recognition and appear more manageable. By using each part more — for instance by calling on your creative part and recognising the intuitive voice in every situation — you will increase your thinking skill. Frequently, halfway through a technique, the problem will evaporate. It is no longer an issue, because your perceptions have changed, based on a different way of looking at things. So this is also a way to determine which are the real problems, which might need a longer period of unconscious 'incubation', and those that simply call for better thinking. Get to know your inner team. Instead of your inner parts working in conflict, they can be made to work *for* you They are your personal inner resource to help you achieve all your goals.

7

Creating Choices

▼

THE MORE CHOICES we have, the more we can take control of our lives. And we create choices by first seeing things from different points of view, different perspectives. One choice is no choice. Two choices might be a dilemma. We need three or more choices to give us the power to do what we want. NLP provides new ways to stimulate the necessary thinking to open up more choices. These techniques help you to do what you are already more than capable of doing, to think in a creative, holistic way about any problem or issue.

Depending on the meaning we give to a circumstance or event, we will feel differently about it, and behave accordingly. Moreover, if we look at something in a different light, it often takes on a different meaning, and so affects us differently. We have a choice, of course, as to the meaning we give to any event, or the particular perspective from which we view it.

We create choices by seeing things from different perspectives. We have already met the terms *associated* and *dissociated* — seeing things as if through our own eyes, and as if through someone else's. The associated viewpoint is also known in NLP as the *first perceptual* position. If we see things from the perspective of the person we are relating to, this is known as the *second perceptual position*. The *third perceptual position* is when we view both people in an interaction as if we were a third party — an outside observer. This third position offers an infinite choice of viewpoints. So far, we have seen how important it is to get inside a visualisation in an associated way — that is, to see things from the first perceptual position. But when it comes to opening up new perspectives, and generating choices, we need to be able to switch to other positions.

REFRAMING

A very old Chinese Taoist story describes a farmer in a poor country village. He was considered very well-to-do because he owned a horse which he used for ploughing and for transport. One day his horse ran away. All his neighbours exclaimed at how terrible this was, but the farmer simply said 'Maybe.' A few days later the horse returned and brought two wild horses with it. The neighbours all rejoiced at his good fortune, but the farmer just said 'Maybe.' The next day the farmer's son tried to ride one of the wild horses; the horse threw him and broke his leg. The neighbours all offered their sympathy for his misfortune, but the farmer again said 'Maybe.' The next week conscription officers came into the village to take young men for the army. They rejected the farmer's son because of his broken leg. When the neighbours told him how lucky he was, the farmer replied 'Maybe.'

The meaning of any event depends on its context or *frame*. Thus, changing the frame of reference round an event or statement to give it another meaning is known in NLP as reframing. The simple event of receiving a telephone call can be a nuisance if you have just settled down to watch a favourite television programme, but to a lonely person who has not spoken to a soul all day it can be most welcome. Changing the frame, or context, changes the meaning. Getting measles might be a trauma for a young executive about to do her first overseas trip, but rather gratifying for a ten-year-old who likes the idea of some time off school. So, depending on the context of any event, it will be given a different meaning. And that meaning, rather than the actual experience, will dictate how we react and feel.

We can also think about some aspect of the situation, that is the *content* of an experience, and similarly change its meaning. In the case of the ten-year-old, the experience might involve a visit to the doctor that the child is not so happy about, or missing a school sports day that he has been looking forward to. Any aspect of an experience, as well as the context in which it occurs, is liable to affect its meaning. Politicians and advertisers frequently reframe situations by directing our attention to features or statistics that change the meaning, both in content ('never mind the price, look at the shine') and context (what we spend on other goods, historical trends or world comparisons).

The army general who reassured his troops by saying: 'We are not retreating, we're just advancing in another direction' knew about reframing, and its effect on morale. Successful businesses have learned to constantly reframe their markets and products. A 'problem' factory effluent can be reframed to become a profitable by-product. The seed of an idea from an irate customer becomes an opportunity to improve quality or service. Or you can reframe your career path and promotion prospects. This might be as simple as seeing things in a longer time context, so that the 'pain' of the short term is more than balanced by the longer-term benefits; bosses come and go; few of our major problems of a year ago exist today, and many of them we cannot even recall.

Even the drudgery of commuting can be successfully reframed. The extra time spent on the train can be converted into extra knowledge; learning another language; gaining a degree or other qualification; valuable, systematic reading to enhance your job knowledge and career; writing a book; learning about a new hobby or some completely new interest; meditating; relaxing; meeting new people. As well as the tangible benefits wise use of commuting time can bring, the reframe can change your attitude to it, so that you no longer suffer the resentment, frustration and other negative emotions that you once did. Or you might reframe your three or four hours a day commuting time in some other productive way, and decide to work much nearer home, or move home, or use it as part of your normal sleeping time. The choice is yours.

Reframing gives you more control of your life by making you more aware of alternatives. It can work wonders with difficult children. A distasteful or boring task can become an exciting game, just by adding the ingredient of imagination. Children's stories are full of reframes — from the Ugly Duckling to Cinderella. Meaning is changed. More than anything else, seeing something differently gives a choice of meaning — a meaning that can be empowering rather than disempowering, motivating rather than demotivating, pleasurable rather than painful. So the skill of reframing, although we all have it already in some measure, is well worth cultivating and using for specific outcomes.

By reframing personal behaviour we can change the meaning we give it. If you want to reframe the statement 'I wish I could stop doing . . .' you could ask yourself: 'When might this behaviour be useful?' That is, think of a different context that would change its meaning. For example, if you come across as terse and abrupt in conversation, this could be an asset when you have to say 'no' to some unreasonable request — and many people will indeed envy your ability to say bluntly what you want to say. Because any behaviour depends on a context for its meaning, considering alternative contexts will enable you to see the situation more objectively, and will probably make you feel better.

Another statement might be 'I panic when asked to do anything, like make a speech or act a simple charade in front of a group.' In this case you could ask: 'What is the positive value of this behaviour?' or 'How else could I describe what happens?' Positively, it might be the degree to which adrenaline prepares you to give your best. (Thousands of entertainers are familiar with what they might describe as 'mild panic' before a performance.) It probably also means that you make up for it by preparing more fully than a 'natural' performer. It might be that you are the only person who realises anything is wrong! And if the experience is a rare one, maybe you just don't get enough practice to feel confident. What does it mean? That you are hopeless? That you are like most people? Or that you need to join a local club of some sort and get a bit of risk-free practice?

A lot of public presenters and entertainers have little tricks that help them to reframe otherwise frightening situations. One famous orator would visualise his audience naked, another wearing cheap party hats, and so on. If you are intimidated by formal business suits, imagine your audience in scruffy, torn jeans. Or you can make them fat or thin, old or young — even children in highchairs. Your experience with earlier visualisation exercises can be used to reframe any situation you wish. And once reframed, it is impossible to feel the same way about it. Just try to feel the same way addressing a group of 15-month-old toddlers as you would top executives. And the more you can introduce different, more helpful frames to what you do, the more you will be able to handle challenging situations naturally.

Give this a try. Think of a big mistake you made during the last year. The chances are that when you think about it you will quickly take on the negative, unpleasant state you experienced at the time. You might have a sinking feeling, or a feeling of hopelessness or fear. This mistake is now part of your life in a disempowering way. Now, as you think back to the mistake, see if you can reframe its meaning. Try changing the context, and then the content. See it in different ways. Focus on one aspect of it, then another. It might be that, with hindsight, it has taught you some lessons, and so can be of benefit. Maybe you have already benefited from the event. You can add to your creativity by imagining how other people you know might have reacted to and learned from such an experience. Would everyone consider it the big mistake you did? Would some people get over it more quickly, or even view it in a different way altogether? Are there other, new lessons you can learn as you see what happened in a different light? Try and separate yourself from the behaviour, in order to see it objectively. As you do this, it will have a less emotional effect on you. You can even make a disempowering memory into an empowering one by reframing it.

Six-step reframe

Reframing has been applied successfully to all kinds of human behaviour problems. All behaviour, as we have seen, has some purpose, or intent, at least in a particular context. Although much of our behaviour can be changed by visualisation, some secondary benefit may still be gained by the actions or behaviour. So in due course these intents, which may well be unconscious ones, may arise again to affect our behaviour. If smoking, for instance, makes a person feel relaxed and confident, this positive intent needs to be fulfilled in some other, better way. Whatever the pain associated with a negative habit, there is usually some secondary gain that has to be taken into account. If not, the habit will persist, as everything we do is to gain pleasure or avoid pain.

A 'six-step reframe' takes this into account by identifying all the underlying intentions behind the unwanted behaviour. In the previous chapter we met our inner team, and the exercises identified the different intentions of each different part. This involves communicating with yourself, and is a highly subjective, right-brain way of thinking. You can now use that skill in this reframing exercise which is particularly effective in bringing about permanent changes to unwanted behaviour. It has been used a lot for smoking, overeating, nail-biting and all manner of habits that people want to rid themselves of — but which seem to be out of the control of the conscious mind.

This technique is usually used with someone else, because when we are addressing unconscious parts of ourselves an observer can often see physiological changes that we are not aware of. These non-verbal signals can be an effective way to communicate otherwise unknown intentions. Having said this, if you were able to do the inner team exercise, you can probably also benefit from doing this one on your own. If you do work closely with a friend or spouse, you will each build up your knowledge and skill in the techniques generally, benefiting mutually. When working with someone else, you need not divulge the content of the reframe — the actual nature of the behaviour you want to change. Instead, you can refer to the behaviour as X or Y, for instance.

The technique involves getting a 'yes' or 'no' signal from inner parts of you. A 'signal' can be any visual, auditory or kinesthetic sensation. It might be the indefinable 'gut feeling', an increase in temperature in your hand, a buzzing in your ear, an inner voice, some visual image, or a change in breathing. To illustrate this, imagine a lorry driver who is very sensitive to his vehicle. He is usually aware of slight differences in tyre pressure, engine or transmission noise, and the state of his load. Although he will happily engage in conversation while driving, he is unconsciously monitoring, through all modalities (including smell) the state of his vehicle. Although unconscious of these until they change, and are therefore significant, with some thought and concentration he might be able to describe these different signals.

In the same way it is possible to interpret messages from our unconscious self. In some cases it is easy and a person will quickly feel a 'yes' or a 'no', perhaps hearing or seeing the word mentally. An observer or partner will sometimes see the person nodding or shaking their head (clearly signifying a yes or no) several seconds before the 'yes' or 'no' is actually verbalised. Facial and other changes might be just as obvious to an observer, who is left in no doubt as to whether a positive or negative response is being received. We have already seen the wide range of physiological changes that a change in mental state produces. On your own, just be aware of any mental or physiological change. Each of us has a unique, personal way of thinking and feeling, and there is no substitute for becoming aware of what is going on inside yourself. This just takes practice. You can become as familiar with your internal subjective world as you are with the external objective world. A response can be tested by asking the part responsible for the behaviour to communicate 'yes', then 'no', so you can distinguish between the two.

Now think of a recurring experience, habit or behaviour that you cannot change, but would like to. Then follow the six steps carefully.

1. **Identify the habit or pattern of behaviour you want to change.**

2. **Establish communication with the part of you that generates the behaviour.** Get into the alpha state, and ask this question of your unconscious: 'Will the part of me that generates so-and-so behaviour be willing to communicate with me (consciously)?' Now ask that part to give a signal, intensifying it to communicate 'yes' and diminishing it to communicate 'no'.

3. **Separate the intention from the behaviour.** The unwanted behaviour is only a way to achieve some positive intention. Thank the part for its willingness to cooperate. Now ask it if it is willing to let you know what it has been trying to do by generating the behaviour. Having received a positive response, note what benefits this behaviour has provided for you in the past. You might want

to write down what you learn at this stage. Also establish that this part is willing to try out new behaviour that will bring about its intention.

4. **Create alternative behaviour to satisfy your intention.** The next step is to find some new behaviour that will satisfy your intention as well or better than the undesired behaviour. Here you need to call on your creative part to come up with the ideas, just as you did in Chapter 6. Politely contact your creative part, thank it for its willingness to help, and ask it to generate three alternative behaviours as good as or better than the one you want to change. Give it time, and ask if it is willing to reveal these to you. If you are working with someone else, you can ask the creative part to give a signal as each of the three alternatives has been thought of, so that you know the process is working well. When you know that three have been identified, ask for them to be spoken aloud. Again you may wish to write down what you learn during this stage.

5. **Get the part of you that is responsible for the old behaviour to be responsible for generating the new behaviour.** You can start by asking whether the three new behaviours are at least as effective as the old one. If not, go back to your creative self and ask for more ideas. Now check that the part of you contacted in Step 2 is willing to take responsibility for generating the new behaviour in appropriate situations.

6. **Do an ecology check.** You came across this back in Chapter 2 when clarifying your goals. Ask if there are any parts of you that object to what

you have just negotiated, and request their support. If you do not get agreement, go back to the beginning. This time incorporate the part of you that objected in the negotiation, calling on your creative part for ideas as to how to overcome the objection. Finally, do some future pacing. Step into the future and imagine a situation that would have triggered the old behaviour, but experience it using one of your new choices in its place. Then step into a different situation, and experience using the second suggested behaviour, and then the third.

Each step is important, and if you do not achieve each interim objective, you will have to go back one or more steps. But each skill you gain will build up your overall effectiveness. For instance, once you have learned to communicate subjectively with a 'familiar' part of you, say the critic, you can use your sharpened perception to contact other parts. And once you have a line of communication with your creative self, there are all sorts of occasions when you will be able to benefit from its new ideas and insights.

Although the technique calls on your unconscious, it keeps bringing information to a conscious level. It is thus a most powerful means of increasing your self-awareness. You can find out why you have been doing things habitually that you consciously find useless, distasteful or even repugnant, and reframe these in the light of some positive intention. The new ways of behaving will remove the negative associations and emotions linked with your old behaviour. More importantly, they will give you choices. You will still achieve your secondary intentions (maybe to get attention, to escape, or to conform), but you will now have different ways of achieving them, each of which is more acceptable and empowering to your conscious self. Reframing can create congruency between different parts of you that have previously had different intentions. And you did it all consciously — you can achieve control.

POINTS OF VIEW

Another technique used for the same purpose, known as Points of View, helps your flexibility of thought, whilst also providing a helpful problem-solving checklist.

Most problems, as it happens, involve other people. And we commonly express problems as beliefs — 'She just doesn't understand,' 'He will never change' — or as goals: 'I really want to get to know him better.' These are, of course, points of view. And we can generate more points of view by making up sentences incorporating the following common words:

good, bad, right, wrong, stupid, smart, better, worse

Using the first example, 'She just doesn't understand,' these words can be used in the following forms to elicit new points of view:

It's good that she doesn't understand **because** she might not be able to face things.
It's bad that she doesn't understand **because** it's ruining our relationship.
It's right that she doesn't understand **because** she

doesn't have all the facts.

It's wrong that she doesn't understand **because** that's what she's paid to do.

It's stupid that she doesn't understand **because** she is coming off worse.

It's smart that she doesn't understand **because** she can't be held responsible.

It's better not to understand **than** do what she does out of malice.

It's worse not to understand **than** not to even listen.

The 'trigger' words, **good, bad,** etc, are used to help you come up with widely differing points of view, so the exercise involves using language in a constructive way, making it your servant rather than your master. You can be as ingenious and creative as you wish when making up sentences. After all, a predictable or very logical response has probably already been considered by the problem-owner, yet the problem remains. And if one or two viewpoints seem too unlikely you can just move on to the others. Whether you come up with a 'eureka' insight, or just feel less emotive about the person or issue, you are developing flexibility of thought, and learning to take control of your beliefs and behaviour.

SLEIGHT OF MOUTH

Another technique for creating choices involves responding to any problem or statement from a different angle. For example, the problem might be stated as: 'I'll never make my monthly sales target.' Here are the different perspectives, or categories of response:

- **positive outcome**: 'So you'll try harder next month' or 'But you do seem to be spending more time with the boys' or 'What about getting on that new course?' This type of response suggests a positive or optimistic outcome that might result from the situation, however unlikely or far-fetched. The aim is not to provide ready-made solutions, but to open up new angles and remove any mental blinkers.

- **negative outcome**: 'So your job might be on the line?' This suggests a pessimistic consequence.

- **different outcome**: 'Are you bothered about what Cath will think?' or 'Does this mean the weekend break is off?' Think of any different outcome.

- **a metaphor**: 'It's just like missing a bus, there's always another one behind' or 'Every cloud has a silver lining' or 'Thomas Edison missed a few hundred targets.' Again, the metaphor does not provide a ready-made solution. It just opens up another viewpoint that can easily be visualised. In any event, the meaning and associations of any metaphor, or story, will differ from person to person.

- **a different timeframe**: 'Maybe next month will be better' or 'How do your annual figures look?'

- **a model of the world**: 'I suppose life is full of missed targets.' This lifts the problem to a general, perhaps philosophical, level.

- **personal values and criteria**: 'Is that a worry for you?' or 'What's important about that for you?' This focuses on the person, seeking to expose any underlying values and beliefs that are involved.

- **set a further outcome**: 'It's not missing your target that's important, but worrying about it.'

- **redefine**: 'Maybe the target is unrealistic' or 'You seem to be very sensitive about your performance.'

- **chunk up**: 'Are you failing in other ways?' Chunking up takes the problem to a higher, and possibly more general, level. We shall look at chunking later.

- **chunk down**: 'Which orders are the problem?' or 'How do you get your leads?' or 'How much will you miss it by?' Chunking down goes the other way, breaking the problem down into progressively smaller chunks.

- **counter-examples**: 'Do we ever get better without failing sometimes?'

- **positive intention**: 'It sounds as though you want to do well.'

You will notice that some of these overlap, although there are subtle differences. For example a positive intention (on the part of the problem-stater) and a positive outcome response (to the problem) might be very similar but still offer slightly different perspectives. At the same time, each category of response might open up several angles — there is no limit, for instance, to counter-examples, chunking up and down, or metaphors that might be used to elicit new perspectives. So you have scores of chances to crack open an otherwise intractable problem, thus creating more choices.

You will also note that some skill and ingenuity is needed to think of more creative responses. As with any technique involving creativity, there is no 'programmable' system, no left-brain logic to follow. This technique, known as sleight of mouth (alluding to the conjuror's sleight of hand), helps to stimulate right-brain creativity.

As with most NLP exercises, you can use this on your own as well as with other people. Although you might not get as many bright ideas, the process demands that you look at your problem in many different lights, and this will almost certainly enable you to see things differently. You might be surprised at your ingenuity in coming up with suggestions that, only with hindsight, may seem 'obvious'.

This technique can be used with any problem — professional or personal, big or small. It can easily be amended to goal achievement. The 'problem' becomes 'I want this but don't have it' or 'I am at x and want to be at y.' Besides being fun, it is very powerful and potentially life-changing. Some of the categories, such as chunking and metaphors, have been developed in their own right as major problem-solving tools in large companies.

If you have difficulty coming up with any response, just move on to the next heading. You can always come back to it later; sometimes we need to 'incubate' new angles for a while before we get insightful responses. You have plenty of angles to work from and just one good idea can unblock a problem.

Chunking

The general principle of chunking is simple. An issue, or subject, is viewed in larger or smaller 'chunks'. In considering dogs, for example, we can think upward to consider animals, then further upward to consider living things, and so on to a cosmic level. This is termed 'chunking up'. Alternatively, we can 'chunk down' from dogs to spaniels, or Rover (a particular spaniel), then further down to Rover's paw. We can also chunk sideways, so dogs might give us cats or horses. And because our associations will be subjective, they might be lateral in more senses than one. For instance, a sideways chunking of cats might be *Starlight Express* (a musical show, as is *Cats*), which might be chunked upwards to Andrew Lloyd Webber (the composer), and then on to musicians, famous people, and so on. *Starlight Express*, on the other hand, can be chunked down to a specific song or singer, or some other detail, or sideways to *West Side Story*, or, again more laterally, to the *Flying Scotsman* — a famous railway locomotive.

The process of chunking maintains some link with an original concept or issue, but introduces new associations, letting you see things from many different vantage points. The randomness and subjectivity introduce the lateral thinking needed to open up an issue. Very little creativity is needed to use the technique. It is as simple as a word association party game and calls on the right-brain subconscious in an instinctive rather than a logical way.

Going back to the earlier example of missing a monthly sales target, one response would be to chunk up by asking: 'Is this sort of failure common?' or 'Are there other goals you are not achieving?' or, even higher, 'Life is full of missed targets.' Chunking down, you might ask: 'How much will you miss it by?', 'Which orders are the problem?' or 'Have you called in to see so-and-so recently?' Typically, chunking up will put the problem into perspective (is it *really* a life or death matter?) and chunking down will provide focus, making the ordeal more manageable. In both cases the effect will be to unblock an impasse. Responses can be in the form of statements or questions, but not criticism or solutions. And the problem-owner should reach the solution himself and, if need be, take responsibility for implementation. More than one solution might emerge, and the best one can then be chosen.

The chunking technique has some very wide applications. Take Sue and Mary. Sue is a committed vegetarian and Mary an unashamed meat-eater. Although otherwise the best of colleagues, they can hardly bear to be near each other in the staff canteen, as both are so set in their respective ways. In negotiation or mediation you could ask each party: 'Do you respect people's rights to have their own beliefs?' (chunking up, to gain common, higher ground). When consensus is achieved at this higher, less emotive, level questions can be chunked down to include the other party: 'Do you respect *Mary's* right to have her own beliefs?' Another upward chunk might be: 'Do you get on all right with Sue as a colleague?' (higher common ground again), or the chunking might embrace sports, hobbies and interests that both enjoy. Chunking laterally might prompt you to ask Mary: 'Do you have other friends and family who do/don't eat meat, and how do you manage socially?' Then you could chunk downwards: 'Do you always eat meat?' to which the reply might well be: 'Of course not. I like salads.' Another chunking down response might be to ask: 'Could you manage to eat with each other, say, once a week?' or 'Might the choice of food be less blatantly vegetarian or carnivorous on the occasions you eat together?' It turns out, of course, that the problem is not intractable, and that Sue and Mary can eat together happily every Thursday when Mary enjoys her salad and Sue a vegetarian burger. This is an exercise in right-brain creativity, but using the comfortable left-brain logical structure that chunking provides.

Constant exploratory chunking up and down is a device used (often unknowingly) by top negotiators. It usually finds common ground, an acceptable compromise, or even a win-win solution. In commercial negotiations both sides have the same higher-level interest in wanting to do a deal, to maintain good relationships, to be seen as reasonable, and so on — all of which can be achieved by chunking up to whatever level is necessary. At the same time it might be a very small part of the deal which is causing the problem. In this case you will have to chunk down to find the difficulty, and show it in the context of the bigger picture. The chunking technique is powerful and has a lot of applications. It illustrates that, although you cannot generate insights at will, you can do a lot to stimulate them.

As well as its use in negotiation, the technique can be used as an effective problem-solving skill. Simply exchange the polarised views of Sue and Mary for the two or more apparently irreconcilable factors that most problems comprise. It does require some creativity to spot chunked associations, or new angles. And you will need to practise before useful, creative ideas start coming in quantity and quality. However, this process is more likely to bring conclusive results than just sitting waiting for inspiration. It's also a useful tool for harnessing all the relevant data, and therefore appeals to left-brain, logical thinkers.

Reversals

This takes the 'new angle' approach as far as possible — in fact it rotates the problem 180 degrees! 'True statements' are simply reversed. The reversals are then imagined to be true and examined to see what issues or opportunities they open up. For example, in a business setting, where the technique has been used very successfully, 'We are the market leader' would be reversed to 'We are not the market leader.' Imagine this reversal is true and consider what issues or opportunities it raises. In the famous case of Avis car rentals, who were second to Hertz, not being the market leader meant 'We try harder' and suggested a powerful new marketing thrust worth millions of dollars.

Reversal statements stimulate radical thinking. By definition, the technique does not allow any possibility to be excluded from consideration. It can be used to find new opportunities as well as for problem-solving, so the initial true statements need not be confined to 'problems'. In the case of cheap biros, for example, 'We make pens' would reverse to 'We don't make pens.' The issue thus raised might be 'What on earth do we make?' and the response, 'Little plastic mouldings that are so cheap you can throw them away.' And within that new perception definition lie all sorts of other plastic throwaway products and a few million francs of profit. The reversal does not produce solutions, it just stimulates a lateral rethink that allows the creative mind the chance to address other questions and issues.

Chunked reversals

A further technique combines the powerful reversal process with chunking. In this case we not only reverse the original statement, we also reverse the chunked perspectives. The way this technique might have been used to market Maltychocs is illustrated below. It starts with the statement: 'Maltychocs make you fat.'

statement and chunking	reversal	issue	so?
Chocolates are bad for you. ↑	Chocolates are good for you.	They are both good and bad - but it's how people perceive them.	Can we make ours seem less bad and more good? Are our chocolalates just like others?
Chocolates make you fat. ↑	Chocolates do not make you fat.	There are bits that do and bits that don't. It's the feeling of guilt - our perception. . .	Can we reduce the guilt a bit?
Maltychocs make you fat. ↓	Maltychocs do not make you fat.	What if they didn't? Can't we make this an opportunity?	Can we change the image, the packaging. . . ?
Parts of Maltychocs make you fat. ↓	Parts of Maltychocs do not make you fat.	What parts? The filling? Can we change anything?	What strengths can we work on? Can we capitalise on the fatness thing?
The chocolate coat is the problem.	The chocolate coat is not the problem.	So should we concentrate on the filling?	We can't do much about the chocolate. The centre isn't that fattening. . . .It's *less fattening* than most of the competition.

And the result of the process? **'Maltychocs: The chocolate with the less fattening centre'** — an insight that is unlikely to have resulted from any sequential, logical thought process. The potential for opening up creative possibilities through this combination of techniques is unlimited. Try it for yourself, replacing 'Maltychocs make you fat' with your own problem-statement.

METAPHORS

One of the 13 Sleight of Mouth responses, you recall, was to introduce a metaphor. The right brain likes to deal in mind pictures, or stories, and can quickly make cross associations on the basis of a few common characteristics. The use of metaphors stimulates the right-brain way of thinking. If you can imagine missing a bus, as in the Sleight of Mouth metaphor earlier, but just losing 15 minutes by waiting for the next one, you can more easily imagine a parallel situation. And once you can imagine an alternative, or another perspective, the original, emotionally charged view is changed. Your new state of mind provides fertile ground for new possibilities, and a solution to the problem is nearer.

The large US company Du Pont used this technique very successfully. They had to develop a fire-resistant fibre that could be dyed without the need for special procedures in customers' mills. The material's tight fibre structure baffled researchers, until one of them applied a metaphor by asking: 'What makes it possible to enter a coal mine?' 'Props that keep the tunnel from collapsing' provided an analogy for changing the molecular structure of the fibre, which then allowed dyes to enter whilst the fibres were 'propped up'. As a result, Nomex, a dyeable, flame-resistant material, is being used for aircraft interiors in a variety of colours.

Metaphors can be drawn from nature. Simple natural phenomena, such as leaves falling off trees in winter, can give us insights into almost any business or personal problem, if the imagination is allowed to explore subtle associations in a childlike way. Nature is often used as a source of metaphors simply because it is so prolific and diverse and, being familiar with it, we can easily 'get the picture'. But metaphors can also be drawn from other industries, from sports or hobbies, well-known works of literature, famous artefacts, or historic events. It is only necessary to divert the language-based, logical left-brain for long enough to allow the visualising right-brain to do what it does best. The choice of metaphors is infinite, as is the range of problems to which they can be applied.

Take the statement: 'We seem to have lost focus on product X; market share has dropped'.

Metaphor chosen:
   Birds fly.
Brainstorming:
   They have a bird's eye view of things. . . .They can see well ahead. . . .They have acute vision. . . .Sometimes they stop flapping their wings and just soar above the world below. But they are exquisitely made . . . super-efficient. . . . They don't waste resources. . . .They practise supreme economy of effort. . . . They seem to know where they are going . . . however far ahead their destination is. . . .They prepare well for the journey . . . .They are ready for any sort of weather. . . .They expect to get to where they are going. . . . They know their enemies. . . . Sometimes they find safety in numbers

. . . at other times in outsmarting predators . . . but always having an acute awareness of everything around . . . the limitless landscape below. Somehow they keep going . . . using every subtle thermal to their advantage . . . not fighting the wind . . . but working with the environment in a successful partnership . . . always maintaining dignity in the magic of flight . . . keeping poise, control, mastery . . . simply being the best at what they do.

Even a blinkered, left-brain thinker should be able to develop a metaphor, then make the mental leap to see associations, and possible lines to explore.

Choose any metaphor you like, be ready to give up on a few before you find some firm new angles to work on. Here are some more examples from the millions all around:

Trees shed their leaves
Tides ebb and flow
Seeds die then grow
Snakes are beautiful
High mountains are barren

There are two important aspects to using metaphorical techniques. First, you should not consciously try to solve the problem; just let the metaphor do its own job. You might suggest a metaphor and the problem-owner, having different personal associations, will interpret it in a quite different way to you, nevertheless getting some benefit. Our individual interpretations of any metaphor are as unique as our different mental maps.

Secondly, do not be satisfied with the first great idea that emerges. Try out a few more metaphors to see whether there is a *better* (cheaper, quicker, more convenient) solution. It is left-brain thinking that usually settles on the first reasonable solution that arises. Creative thinking always believes there is something better.

All these techniques can be used either with a colleague, friend or spouse, in a group, or on your own — in which case you simply address your own problem from the different perspectives, preferably writing down each response to refer back to. Think of any difficult situation in your life, put it into a simple statement, then apply the techniques. Because you are calling on right-brain, creative powers, remember that you will get the best results when you are in a relaxed, alpha frame of mind. You now have a choice of techniques. See which works best for you, using real problems, self-belief issues, and the goals you have already set for yourself. Very often a problem that starts off looking intractable evaporates long before you have exhausted the NLP armoury of problem-solving tools.

8
Winning with Words

▼

THE WORDS WE USE affect the way we think and feel, and the way we think and feel affects the words we use. Our words also have an effect on others, as theirs do on us. It is hard to imagine life without language. In a sense we cannot even think without language, at least in a conscious way. When we think about a problem, we use phrases like 'What if?' or 'If so-and-so, then so-and-so.' If we say inwardly 'I think that will do the trick,' we know what we mean by 'that', having already thought about it — in language. We also know what we mean by 'do the trick', and however we re-express what we mean we will be using more words. So language is part of the very process of thought, as well as, more obviously, the means we use to communicate with others. People who learn another language often talk about their minds being enriched in the process, so it seems that language is even more than the raw material of communication. It is the very stuff of thought.

You can get to know a lot about yourself and others by the words and language you use. 'Anxious' transmits a message to the brain that is different from 'a little concerned' or 'expectant'. The word 'curious' will probably be more useful than the word 'confused'. In the case of a word like 'failure', changing the word to denote learning, feedback or information not only gives beneficial, positive messages to the brain, but avoids personalising an event ('I failed, therefore I am a failure.') It reflects the presupposition that the result of any activity is just feedback in the cybernetic process of goal achievement. If we cannot change the connotations of common words, we have to change the words we use. So you can allow yourself to be misunderstood, but not to be rejected; excited or uncomfortable, but not afraid; stimulated but not irritated. The words you use actually affect the way you feel.

This is an easy and obvious way to get language on your side. Simply decide which words best suit your various goals, although you must include your inner self-talk as well as what you say outwardly. In this chapter you will learn some major NLP techniques based on using language to help bring about what you want. If you have a naturally logical, language-based preference for thinking, and have difficulty visualising outcomes in a subjective way, these techniques should appeal to you.

WORDS CAN BE DANGEROUS

If we aspire to better thinking as the way to get what we want, we will have to get language on our side. Everyday concepts like easy, happy, expensive or red, are thoughts we have had to entrust, for better or worse, to words. Left alone, language can work against us, both in our thinking and in the way we relate to others. You know from your own experience how devastating words can be, especially when they come from someone you care about. How many relationships have been torn apart by cutting words or, rather, the interpretations given to words? This is not a question of the structure of language, but rather how it is used or misused. 'You are just like your father' sounds grammatically correct, but is laden with potential for misunderstanding.

Missing words out

How can words make things go so badly wrong? Think what happens when we use them to communicate. First of all we don't say everything there is to say. In answer to, 'How's the car being going?' or 'What happened about Jane's arm?' our answer can be anything from a very short statement, or a grunt, to an hour or more of animated speech. Most of the time, to survive socially, we err on the side of brevity or incompleteness. In other words, we miss out a lot — there are *deletions* in our language communications. Maybe we assume the gaps will be filled in by the hearer, or that what we have missed out is not relevant. Probably we don't assume anything, but either way there will be a big difference between what we thought we said, and what the hearer thought we said and consequently understood. This goes back to our different maps, which represent our unique thoughts and feelings but do not constitute reality. So the language we use is a further stage removed from our limited maps of reality. It tries to describe a map and not reality; a menu, not the food.

And it does not end there. As well as deleting, we give a *simplified* version of what we know, think and feel. In answer to the common question, 'How's the job going?' we omit most aspects of a comprehensive reply, and then simplify what we do pass on, which opens up the possibility of distorting what we are saying. Then we tend to *generalise* rather than spelling out specifics and the exceptions and qualifications to what we are saying. A reply like 'Fine', 'OK', or 'Terrible', whilst a welcome simplification and generalisation, probably leaves the listener's map little nearer the speaker's and still a long way from 'reality'. So the 'deep structure' of language, as it is referred to in NLP, emerges at the surface in an incomplete, distorted and generalised form. The good news is that it is possible to recognise, from the words and language patterns used, where meaning is distorted or unclear. We can then apply responses that make things clearer. These language patterns and responses are known as the *Meta Model*. Together, they address deletions, distortions and generalisations. It's not important to remember which category the patterns fall into, or the linguistic terms used to describe them. All we need to do is to remember the sorts of words and simple word patterns that signal that something is wrong, and the responses that will usually make the meaning clear.

Making generalisations

Let's start with generalisations. Think about words that raise emotions in otherwise rational people: 'You *never* put things away,' 'You *always* say that.' When you spot a permanent or all-embracing word like 'always', 'never', 'every', 'all' or 'none', you are probably on to a type of generalisation, known in NLP as a *universal quantifier*. These words are deadly, in that they eliminate all (I mean most, or nearly all — you see how ubiquitous the pattern is) the choices and alternatives that better thinking provides. They can end conversations and relationships and induce ulcers. The effective response is to pose the universal word as a question: 'Never?', 'Always?', etc. This usually exposes either an absurdity, or at least an exaggeration. Having raised doubt about the universality or permanence of a statement, you can explore further: 'In what circumstances might you . . .?' or 'Have there been occasions when (e.g.) he *wasn't* late?' Watch out also for cases when the offending words are missing but implied. 'Greek food is greasy' implies that *all* Greek food is greasy, and is another example of a generalisation. Start off by spotting the common words. Then, with practice, you· will begin to spot the hidden patterns.

Another common pattern includes words like 'cannot', 'possible' or 'impossible'. How often have you heard expressions like 'You can't do it like that' or 'That's impossible?' These are just as restricting, if unchallenged, as 'never' or 'always'. They are clarified by asking the question: 'What would happen if you did?' or 'What exactly is stopping you?' By doing this you will be able to distinguish between what is *really* impossible, and what is a type of generalisation termed a *modal operator of possibility*. Getting what you want involves habitually attempting to achieve the impossible.

Its sister pattern is the *modal operator of necessity*, signalled by words like 'should' and 'should not', 'must' and 'must not', or 'ought' and 'ought not'. Again, you can respond: 'What would happen if you did?' A lot of these patterns date back to childhood and social conditioning; they are based on rules which may be long past their sell-by date, yet are still part of our language and thought. 'You should not mix with those people' invites the response: 'What would happen if I did?' Challenging these codes of necessity does not imply rebellion or anarchy, just healthy questioning to see if choices are being unknowingly missed. Note that this and other Meta Model responses do not ask 'Why', but 'What?' or 'How?' The technique explores alternatives without setting any moral agenda, aiming to create alternative points of view, and more possible outcomes.

The final generalisation, known as a *complex equivalence*, is when two statements are put together as though they meant the same thing. For example: 'She must be shattered . . . she has been going all day,' or 'He is not smiling . . . he is not enjoying himself.' In these cases, 'Going all day' is taken to be equivalent to 'being shattered,' and 'not smiling' equivalent to 'not enjoying yourself.' These are more insidious than 'never' and 'can't' as there are no obvious words to watch for. The Meta Model response is: 'How does *this* mean *that?*' Usually it is obvious that the statements are not 'equivalent', so the skill is in spotting the pattern rather than coming up with a clever expose of the misuse of language.

Not being specific

Having considered generalisations, what about *deletions* — the language that is missed out before it becomes a spoken or written communication? Think of the common expression: 'It's a matter of opinion.' What is? The noun 'it' is unspecified. Or 'They are out to get me.' Who are they? 'Things are getting out of hand.' What things? Unspecified nouns are clarified by asking 'Who or what specifically. . . ?'

Not only do we omit specific nouns, we do the same with verbs to equal effect. 'He lost his watch' — How did he lose it? 'She hurt her arm' — How did she hurt it? Many verbs, although they are 'doing' words, leave out a lot. Words like 'travelled', 'helped', or 'worked' do not tell us *how*, so we are left guessing what exactly happened, or what was done. Unspecified verbs are clarified by asking 'How, specifically . . .?'

Sometimes verbs describing an ongoing process are turned into nouns. For example, the verb 'educate' becomes 'education', and 'fulfil' becomes 'fulfilment'. Such nouns seem intangible — you cannot wrap education in a box or lock fulfilment in your garage. So a lot of specific meaning is lost when we use such *nominalisations*, as they are termed. Words like 'respect' can have very different meanings, depending, for instance, on who is respecting whom, and how that respect is demonstrated. Business and government communication is often full of nominalisations, which is why it seems a lot of words are used when little meaning is communicated. To get at the missing information you have to turn the nominalisation back into its verb form, and ask who is doing what, and how are they doing it? Who is educating whom and how? 'She has a bad memory' (a nominalisation) raises the question: 'What does she not remember (the verb), and how does it affect her?'

Drawing comparisons

Comparisons are easily spotted, as words such as 'better', 'best', 'worse' or 'badly' keep occurring. The missing information is invariably what is being compared. You could have done that better' raises the response 'Better than what, or whom?' Are you being compared with somebody else? A three-year-old or a top professional? It makes all the difference. Or with yourself at some time in the past? In which case, was that past performance a 'one-off' or something you have demonstrated many times? In other words, how reasonable and meaningful is the statement? The same line of questioning would apply to things we commonly say to ourselves, such as 'I handled that badly.' Badly compared with whom or what? Your standards or someone else's? These responses should produce the missing information on which better understanding is based.

Making judgements

Close to comparisons are *judgements*. 'John can't manage a large office.' Whose opinion or judgement is this, and upon what criteria is it based? Sometimes there are tell-tale signs of judgemental language patterns, such as adverbs like 'obviously' or 'clearly'. 'Obviously, she has better experience.' To whom is it obvious? 'Clearly, this is a matter for the legal people.' To whom is the judgement, or opinion, clear? Ask for the missing information — who is making the judgement, and on what grounds?

These different types of generalisations and deletions overlap a lot, so if you miss a pattern under one category it might show up as something else. For example, 'John can't manage a large office' is an example of a *modal operator of possibility* (using the giveaway word 'can't) as well as being a *judgement*. Very frequently *comparisons* ('Obviously she has better experience') are also *judgements*.

Making assumptions

The third category of language patterns is *distortions*. These include everyday language that you will be familiar with. Have you ever had someone make a statement like 'You are not sure, are you?' or 'You will not like her.' This is, quite simply, *mind-reading!* And this sort of statement only makes sense if we can read each other's thoughts. These patterns are used when someone thinks they know, without evidence, what another person is thinking or feeling. For example, 'He was delighted, but just didn't show it.' We make these assumptions all the time, often based on non-verbal cues that we think we understand. And, as with all these common language patterns, we are likely to see this one used by others long before we recognise it in ourselves.

There is a fascinating variation on this mind-reading theme. Sometimes we wrongly assume that people *can* read minds, and our language supports this: 'You must have known I would not like that' or 'You knew it would upset me.' *Mind-reading* and *projected mind-reading* are classic recipes for monumental rows.

How do you respond to mind-reading? By asking the question, 'How exactly do you know?' Here's an example:

'Mary does not care about me.'

'How do you know Mary does not care about you?'

'Because she never asks about my work any more.'

The question has elicited another statement, which you will note forms a *complex equivalence* (not asking about work is equivalent to not caring), and also includes the *universal quantifier* word 'never'. By asking the question 'Never?' you can put the work discussion in context. Then you can go on to ask, 'How does this mean that?' which will soon show up any false link between the two statements.

Mistaking the cause

Another distortion that is closely related to the *complex equivalence* is the familiar pattern of *cause and effect*. 'She's been happier since he retired' assumes that 'his retiring' is the cause of her 'being happy'. It is easy to miss these and fall into the trap of assuming a link when no cause and effect relationship exists. You clarify this language pattern by asking: 'How, specifically, does this cause that?'

Presupposing

A close relation to the cause and effect pattern is the *presupposition*. 'Shall we meet at your office or mine?' presupposes that you are willing to meet, and if so at one of those venues. 'Would you like the red or black, Madam?' presupposes that Madam wants one of any hue. Presuppositions can be challenged by asking: 'What makes you believe that. . . ?'

MAKING LANGUAGE WORK *FOR* YOU

How can an understanding of these patterns help you to get what you want? Most of what we do involves other people, and so-called 'successful' people seem to be good communicators. The Meta Model puts interpersonal communication onto another plane, and makes language work *for* rather than against you. You will have seen that there is a standard type of response for every pattern. This does not mean that you always have to use the response in conversation. Merely recognising a pattern and being able to question it mentally will change the way you perceive a situation, how you feel, and how you behave.

Knowing that a language pattern exposes an absurdity means that you will not let it affect you in a serious way — your feelings will be influenced by your interpretation of the statement, and your interpretation will take account of any defect in the language. So you should no longer be fooled by statements that purport to limit what you can or should do. Where you spot a deletion, and you want to gather more information, you are free to make a response and get better understanding, *for your own purposes.* You need not build your own outcomes on untruths, be they presuppositions, mind-reading, or wrong cause and effect relationships. Nor need you be tricked into making meaningless comparisons. When you formulate your goals and plans you will instinctively avoid nominalisations and start using words that have specific, motivating meaning for you.

Talking to yourself

A lot of language is not spoken outwardly. It carries on as self-talk, or inner dialogue, and is the way you think things out, or express what you feel to yourself. Much of this dialogue, which is very close to the surface, and so suffers from the deficiencies of spoken language, takes on the form of Meta Model patterns. So you are as likely to be deluded by your own inner dialogue as by other people's. 'You'll never manage that' might be something you say to yourself far more than it is said by others — and you are more likely to believe yourself. All the Meta Model responses, therefore, also apply to your self-talk. And whereas you need to be very careful in your tone of voice when making a response to someone else, who might be antagonised, you need not be so considerate with yourself. Meta Model skills help you to clarify your own thinking and control your own feelings, as well as helping you to express yourself and negotiate persuasively.

Recognising the patterns

Try these exercises. Find a feature or editorial piece in a popular newspaper or magazine and see how many Meta Model patterns you can spot. Go over the text a few times and each time you will probably find new examples. Then scribble down the questions, or responses you would use, imagining you were addressing the writer of the article, or the people being quoted. Secondly, make a point of listening for these language patterns when at work, at home, or socially. See which ones are the most common. Do not, at this stage, try to pick up your colleagues' every other word, but just listen, identify patterns (even if you cannot put them into a category), and mentally form a response. These exercises will help you to see things in a very different light, will give you greater objectivity, and will mean that you take more control of your feelings, giving you more control of your life and what you do with it.

9

Becoming a Master

NLP PUTS THE CONCEPT OF MASTERY, or human excellence, within everyone's reach. Ways of thinking that were previously associated with genius, or which were thought to result from extraordinary genetic advantage, can now be learned and used by all of us. This 'state of mastery' is one we have all experienced already. For every one of us, there is some area of our life, some skill or ability, that is likely to be viewed by others as excellent, or exhibiting mastery. So the pursuit of excellence becomes both feasible and credible — simply doing more of what we already do.

NATURAL ABILITY

Most people who do something well naturally are not aware of how good they are. For example, some people find it easy to do mental arithmetic — they somehow have a system for doing all sorts of sums 'in their heads', without needing to write anything down, or use calculators. When compared with a computer or some world specialist, their abilities are not so remarkable, but to millions of people, who are not able to manipulate numbers in this way, they seem amazing. They display a level of mastery, or excellence, that is envied. But those who envy them may have natural abilities of their own. For example, let us say that one of these enviers is able to play a musical instrument by ear. She hears a new tune a couple of times and, sure enough, the tune rolls out on the piano as if by magic. It can be remembered at will, and is supplemented by all sorts of harmonies that leave the tone-deaf listener quite stunned.

Examples of people being able to do things well without trying are all around us. You may know a person who somehow can easily relate to children. They are able to keep their attention and humour them in a way that you find impossible even after many years of trying. He or she has, what we might call, a gift. A colleague takes up the game of squash for the first time and in two months has overtaken you on the office league table. (This is after you have been plugging away at the game for ten years — and you are that many years his junior.) Then he goes on to excel in almost every other sport he decides to try. One manager is a 'natural' when it comes to giving public speeches or presentations, although she has far less experience of public speaking than most. One person can do just about any DIY job in the home, another has a natural way with writing letters and reports, another can organise a charitable function flawlessly, or has 'green fingers' in the garden. Whatever the activity, these people display a flair or mastery that is to do with their mental approach, what goes on internally, and probably unconsciously. This is what accounts for their success. And this is what accounts for *your* success — for each of us displays such mastery in one or more areas of our life.

EXCELLENT BEHAVIOUR

There are some common features in this excellent behaviour. Firstly, we are not really conscious of mastery. In the case of so-called natural talents, like music or athleticism, it usually takes a while to realise that not everyone is the same as us. Even Olympic medallists and other world-beaters in different walks of life have difficulty *describing* what makes them so special, or even acknowledging their own mastery — they might put it down to hard work, although they do not seem to struggle and strive to the extent that their less talented competitors do.

Secondly, when we exhibit this sort of mastery, we are not really trying, we just 'let loose', and do, with confidence, what we know we can do well. Again, even at the top level in sport, champions make it look so easy — because to them it *is* easy, in that they are 'unconsciously competent'. But no easier than doing mental arithmetic or fixing a boiler is to a person who displays mastery in those particular areas. There is much truth in the saying: 'The harder I try, the worse I get.' Being conscious of our shortcomings is, of course, part of the learning cycle we met in Chapter 1 and the mastery state is associated with the final unconscious competence stage. Only when we do not need to think consciously about what we are doing can we achieve our best performance. If you think about just what you are doing as you read this book, what happens efficiently at

171

an unconscious level — taking in information, making inner representations, forming an understanding of the subjects you are reading about — will go haywire. Being conscious of any part of the process, from how you convert optical signals into meaning, to how words and syntax are translated into real thought images, would make an otherwise 'easy' task almost impossible. One of the secrets of mastery is learning to *stop trying*.

Thirdly, people's mastery seems to be partly due to their particular thinking strategy. We shall cover strategies later in this chapter. Those we talk to who lead their professions or run big businesses, or exhibit uncanny skills in sport and the arts, or enjoy successful relationships, seem to have developed ways of thinking that account for their success. Even when they are not aware of 'how they do it', by using the universal language of thinking modalities — seeing, hearing and feeling — a little discussion will usually 'elicit' the successful strategy they have, unknowingly, perfected.

Finally, mastery cannot be fully explained in terms of factors beyond our control, such as ethnic origin, educational opportunities, genetic serendipity or personality traits. We all excel at something, and have the potential to excel in many more fields. We are all masters. Once you gain a better understanding of thinking, you can decide in what other areas of your life you would like to exhibit mastery.

BARRIERS TO SUCCESS

What prevents us from excelling? The late Milton H. Erickson did some outstanding work with American Olympic rifle-shooters. He asked each of them the simple question: 'Could you shoot and hit a bull's-eye?' In every case the answer was 'yes'. Then the question was put: 'Could you shoot two, in a row?' Again the answer was yes, but a shaky yes. When the question was raised to three some had to answer no. After five shots the number of confident replies dropped dramatically, until eventually it was clear that none of them believed they could repeat their success more than a handful of times. So the amazing fact was that these leaders in their sport believed they could do something once, but did not believe they could do the same thing again and again. In fact they faced the same belief barriers that might apply to a novice who doubted his or her ability even to hit the target. And, in both cases, the belief limited performance.

If you can do something once, then clearly you are physically able to do it again and again. So, unless you can reasonably blame the wind, an opponent's curse, or your 'tools' (rifle, golf club, cooking utensils, whatever), the problem has to be in the brain — how you think and what you believe. And this is exactly what every major study has confirmed. A world champion thinks like a champion. A virtuoso pianist thinks like a virtuoso. The 'difference that makes the difference' is in the mind.

We might be tempted to blame the Olympic rifle-shooters for not being able to believe in their ability to repeat a winning shot, but we are all guilty of the same self-limitation in all sorts of areas. We can all think back to occasions when we have acted with mastery — somehow everything went right and we just could not fail. In other words, we have also experienced the odd bull's-eye. Yet, like the top rifle-shooters, we do not believe that we can repeat our performance again and again. NLP techniques enable you to do what you can already do more consistently, and to transfer successful thinking strategies to other areas of your life.

FALSE FRIENDS

There are a few very common barriers to success, ways in which our negative beliefs show up in everyday life and prevent us from achieving mastery. Paradoxically, some of these barriers are used by well-meaning friends wishing to help us, so they might be called 'false friends'.

Try harder

Logically, this is sound advice. Unfortunately, it simply does not work! The fastest learning period of our lives is the first few years, and the most effective learning happens when we are enjoying the learning experience, unaware of any 'trying'. Learning, and indeed achieving, mastery is a natural process. People who, in later life, are unable to swim, ride a bicycle or do some activity most others consider simple, often remember unpleasant experiences when they were made to try harder, and in particular were made to feel self-conscious about their efforts. In these and many other cases, trying harder not only prevented natural learning but also created a life-long negative self-image about that activity. This is not to say that some effort may not be needed. But if what we do does not work, the secret of learning is to do something *different*, rather than to try harder and harder at the thing that failed. A truer friend might advise: 'Try something different.'

Be perfect

A lot of our negative beliefs stem from the social conditioning that we have to be perfect. We must have the perfect body, the perfect job, the perfect house, the perfect relationship — some ideal that, with a moment's rational thought, we would realise was unobtainable in the real world. And yet this desire for perfection pervades our beliefs and behaviour, preventing us from achieving what we can realistically aim for. Success and mastery is a journey rather than a specific destination like perfection. We never stop learning or making mistakes. By applying the goal clarification tests in Chapter 2 you can expose such a false friend without short-changing yourself about what you are able to achieve.

Try to please someone

This advice, like many other false friends, probably comes from an 'authority', some person, institution or code of values, and so appears irrefutable. Again, as a basis for successful behaviour, it is not true or helpful. How many times have you heard (or said to yourself) 'Whatever I do or say he/she is not pleased'? And the more you seek to achieve results based on such a false premise (the harder you try), the more obvious will be the falsehood. Pleasing someone might be a worthwhile *consequence* of achieving your own goal, and part of the ecology check you did in Chapter 2, but it is not the *way* to personal mastery.

Hurry up

This advice also has its origins in childhood when we were easily conditioned by authority figures. Walk faster, run faster, read faster, finish the job quicker, fax it. It is another form of trying harder, another 'logical' left-brain way to dispense with 'right-brain' insights. If you really have an important deadline and feel yourself 'going under' the last advice you need is to hurry up — it can freeze an already-labouring brain. 'Now just slow down a minute — just relax — there has got to be a way . . .' is far more likely to tap the mental resources you need. If you know where you are going and adopt the right strategy, you will tend to reach your goals in the best way and the quickest time. Apparent delays caused by making mistakes and repeatedly changing your behaviour based on feedback are all an essential part of the success process. They do not slow things down. In achieving any outcome, the direction is more important than the pace.

Be strong

Don't show your weakness. Fight. Compete. This is another false friend which does not produce its intended effect. Our society sets great store by physical or outward strength, and sometimes a 'macho' image. In family or business relationships we are expected to appear strong, however we feel inside. In fact most stories of outstanding human endeavour involve a very different kind of strength, an inner mental or spiritual resilience that overcomes all obstacles despite any lack of outward strength. Paradoxically, this inner strength is more akin to a sense of calmness, congruence and humility rather than the kind of strength our well meaning friends insist we need to have. The human brain is the supreme example of how we can be smart rather than strong and achieve just about anything we set out to achieve. A truer friend might advise: 'Be committed, be aware, be flexible.'

These barriers usually take the form of 'self-talk', the inner dialogue we use when trying to will ourselves to better performance, although their origins are no doubt in actual repeated admonitions. As with real-life friends, you are free to choose them, but also to renounce them. You have the choice, and you can check out for yourself whether these false friends have been empowering or disempowering you to achieve your goals.

WHAT DOES MASTERY FEEL LIKE?

Let us now establish your inherent, probably latent, mastery. Remember that one of the features of excellence is that people often don't recognise it when they have it. Even when it seems that everybody recognises it. In the case of a very common skill, like tying shoelaces, the sophistication of the activity rarely occurs to us. But if you have ever watched a child enviously eyeing a slightly senior friend nonchalantly displaying her lace-tying skills you will know what mastery looks like from the outside. Try to convince a non-swimmer or a non-cyclist that it is 'easy', 'anybody can do it, you don't even have to try,' and you will begin to see what natural mastery is all about. Half the population might be good at DIY, yet, without realising it, they are able to do things that seem almost superhuman to others.

If you are still in doubt, think of everything you do throughout your day. Don't miss things out — like shaving, or making coffee, or driving to work, or getting the children somewhere on time, or reading half a novel in a couple of evenings. Then try to come to terms with the awesome complexity of what you have accomplished — the hundreds of coordinated muscle movements, the chemical changes in your body, the manual dexterity, the way you can drive miles without being conscious of the journey, while mentally solving problems or holding a conversation. Then take your mind back. Just because you have forgotten the ten thousand 'unsuccessful' body movements that climaxed in your first faltering steps at one year old, the magic of the skill is not undervalued. And after a million attempts at successfully communicating in your mother tongue, you can now hold a conversation without realising the vast learning or the outstanding human achievement involved. Not to mention working the video recorder!

So mastery is universal. And, of course, it is relative to other people. You will be looked on by others as displaying some special aptitude or skill, and you in turn will look on others with similar admiration. This applies to the same skill (for example, different levels in the same craft, musical ability or sport, or universal activity such as driving a car) as well as between different skills. In the former case you will probably look on the expert in the same way as a complete novice looks on you, and in the latter case we all tend to view with awe a skill that is alien to us. But in other ways mastery is unique and personal. There are some things that only you can do in the special way you do them. So think it over and choose some past action or event that illustrates your mastery. A time when you had that sense of complete confidence in yourself. A time when, without really trying, you excelled at what you were doing.

Now relive that experience with all the intensity possible. Use the techniques you used in earlier exercises, going successively through each modality, seeing, hearing and feeling. Note the submodalities, referring back if necessary to your checklist on pages 66/7. In particular, try to regain the overall feeling you had at the time — be it a sense of lightness, a feeling in your stomach, whatever. Then choose an area in your life in which you want to experience greater confidence. For this exercise you need not select an area where you feel 'hopeless', but rather one where you know there is lots of room for improvement, in particular one which you will have the opportunity to practise in the future. Having made your choice, relive *this* experience, and identify the submodalities. Then compare the submodalities in the mastery state with those in the 'mediocre' state. Give yourself plenty of time for this, and get into a relaxed alpha state in which it will be far easier to visualise and notice differences.

TRANSFERRING MASTERY

The next stage is to transfer the mastery submodalities to the situation you want to change. If the images are bigger and brighter in the mastery state, change the situation you want to improve to mirror these submodalities. Importantly, if the mediocre image is not 'associated' (that is, you do not see things through your own eyes) but the mastery experience is, then make this important change. Go through each of the submodalities and wherever there is a difference, substitute the effective, mastery pattern. Finally, whilst re-experiencing the situation you wish to change, bring back the *feeling*, all the kinesthetic submodalities that you have identified and become familiar with in your mental journeys.

There is another important element you can add if you wish. What if your memory of excellence is not as good as you would like it to be, especially when comparing yourself with others? As well as visualising your own successful experience, you can also imagine someone else doing the activity, even a top professional you have seen on television but have never met. You just need to call upon your powers of imagination. While doing this, become associated with the scene — that is, put yourself *in* the person's place, imagine yourself doing things the way they do them, and feeling the way they feel.

The same modelling technique can be applied to the activity at which you wish to improve. As well as switching submodalities, you can visualise someone else doing the activity, and again becoming associated. No doubt you will choose a different 'model', someone who excels at this particular activity. Imagining you are someone else can produce remarkable changes, even without a great deal of skill in manipulating the changes in submodalities.

These basic techniques can be applied whenever you need to associate a better state of mind with any activity. If you have difficulty in identifying submodalities for the purpose of the changes, you may need to choose events or activities that arouse very different feelings. So, for example, by choosing some activity you were *afraid* to do, rather than just mediocre at, and which was unpleasant to recall, there would be more likelihood of spotting different submodalities. In this case it is likely that the imagery would be dim, distant, perhaps even in black and white — obviously different from the clearly focused, colourful imagery of a mastery experience.

It is this combination of submodalities, in all three main representation systems, that makes you feel *afraid* at the very thought of some activities. Changing the submodalities will change how you feel, and thus how you perform. The content — the activity or skill itself — does not account for the different way you feel. It is our individual, unique associations with a particular activity, person, place or memory that create how we feel about it — our state — and what we believe about ourselves in that role. So the main reason for our differing performance in different skills or activities is the different perceptions we have about them; in other words, the pattern of our thoughts rather than the content of the skill or activity.

If you find it quite easy to recognise differences in submodalities as you move from one memory to another, you are free to tackle behaviour in stages, first seeking mastery in areas where you are already relatively confident, and then building one success on another. It will be easier to practise new behaviour if you apply the techniques in this stage-by-stage way. If, for instance, you already regularly chair a meeting, or present a monthly report, you will easily be able to practise your visualised mastery in these familiar settings. You can then move on to bigger and different kinds of challenge. So put all your techniques into practice as soon as possible without turning your life upside down.

STRATEGIES FOR MASTERY

One of the mastery factors we identified at the beginning of the chapter was being able to copy the thinking strategy adopted by outstanding people. The components of any thinking strategy are the five senses, the modalities that feature in NLP techniques and allow us to account for differences from person to person, and between one behaviour and another. But, having identified the modalities at work, then further identified the submodalities, we need to identify the sequence in which these occur. This order is critical to the overall success of the strategy. The same applies to the words we use. The phrases 'The book is in my hand' and 'My hand is in the book' have very different meanings, but this is only made clear in the language by syntax, or the order in which the words are used.

A useful analogy is baking or cooking. You can have all the ingredients and their quantities right, but unless you add them and do what has to be done in the right order you will not produce the outcome that the expert cook produces. So NLP pays a lot of attention to successful people's strategies, both externally (what they do, and the order in which they do things) and internally (how they think, and the order in which those thought processes occur). Mastery, in any area, is accounted for by a *strategy*. If repeated in the individual, the same strategy produces the same results consistently. When masterly behaviour is modelled or copied by someone else, similar outcomes can also be achieved. So, first we have to identify a successful strategy, to a necessary level of detail, then use it to change our own behaviour, and thus the results we achieve.

This concept revolutionises the whole field of self-development. A master might have taken many years to reach a level of excellence, unaware of the internal strategies that he or she has evolved over the period. Whereas we can model the person in order to achieve similar results without years of hard labour and 'trying'. Time may be needed to reach the required level of physical fitness, coordination or conditioning, depending on the nature of the skill. But this is usually a small fraction of the overall time it has taken to develop the mastery strategy. And it is the strategy itself that is the key to what your brain is able to accomplish. If mastery is the combination lock on a vault full of treasure, you need to know the right numbers, and get them in the right order. If you do, you will manage to open the vault door every time. The syntax, or strategy, is the master key to getting what you want.

We all have strategies for everything we do in an automatic way. It is very rare for people to be aware of how they think at times when they perform outstandingly. Even with careful 'elicitation' some people are not sufficiently familiar with their basic thought processes (the representation system and its submodalities) to be able to communicate the ingredients and order of their successful strategies. But these combination locks are waiting to be cracked. Already, work on strategy in areas such as spelling is proving to be of universal benefit. It has been shown that mastery in some activities, and spelling is one of them, follows a standard pattern. In other words, all good spellers follow the basic strategy, and anyone adopting the strategy will improve their spelling ability.

Mastery strategy for spelling

So what has NLP research discovered about spelling? The secret to good spelling is being able to store words in a visual way. The skill does not lend itself to kinesthetic representation which would involve 'feeling' each word, although, as we shall see, feeling is certainly part of the process. One might expect an auditory thinker to do well at spelling, as we often tend to say words as we spell them. But there are so many words where the sound and spelling differ that to relate spelling to sounds makes it harder rather than easier. Somehow the process would have to reconcile the different pronunciation and spelling of words like 'rough', 'bough', 'dough', 'cough', 'ought' and hundreds of others to make any sense at all. Specifically, the best way to remember how to spell a word is to visualise it, a little up and to your left in your mind's eye, and store that picture. When you see the word again, it will 'look right' or 'feel right', or, if spelled incorrectly, it will 'look wrong' or 'feel wrong'. All top spellers that have been researched use some form of visualisation, usually looking up or straight ahead as they recalled a word, then down as they confirmed (kinesthetically) that it felt right.

This visualisation strategy was tested on students at the University of Moncton, New Brunswick, in Canada, using nonsense words the students had never seen before. An immediate improvement of 20 per cent in spelling performance was recorded where students had been asked to look up and to their left when visualising, but only a 10 per cent improvement in those asked to use any eye position. Those asked to spell in whatever way they had been used to showed no change at all. And, interestingly, a group asked to visualise the words whilst looking down and to the right (the kinesthetic eye access position) actually *worsened* their spelling scores. This strategy has been used successfully with children labelled as dyslexic.

If you want to improve your spelling here is a basic strategy to follow:

- First, think of anything that feels familiar and comfortable.

- Next, for a few seconds, look at the word you wish to remember.

- Look away from the word, up and to your left, and picture the word as best you.can as you try to spell it in your mind.

- Look back at the word, noticing any letters you have missed and repeat the process until you can picture the whole word.

- To test yourself, after a short break, visualise the word and write it down.

- Now look up at the word again and spell it backwards. This will confirm that you are learning through the best, visual strategy (you simply cannot spell a word backwards if learned phonetically).

Using this basic strategy, you can then develop your own ways to get better and quicker. Try to use submodalities that you know work best for you. You may, for instance, want to see the words in your favourite colour, perhaps as large 3-D letters, or written as if on a flip chart with a marker pen, or in neon lights. You can give special treatment to particularly difficult words so they will stick in your memory. You might also like to place the words on a familiar background, such as your lounge wall. Break down large words into smaller chunks of three or four letters.

Try a specific word using this strategy, and incorporating the chunking down into smaller parts. The word is 'pyrrhuloxia', which is a bird with a parrot-like bill. First do your chunking down. For example you might divide it as:

pyr rhu loxia

so you are visualising three separate chunks. When first looking at the word, look carefully and precisely. When picturing the word in your mind, be sure to actually *see* it in the way you decide. Don't worry about pronunciation. For the moment your strategy is about spelling. By chunking it down, you just have to remember three little words in a row. Don't forget to do the backward spelling.

If you use the basic strategy as I have described it you will memorise the spelling of this word in less than a minute, and probably in just a few seconds. If you carry out the process again after half an hour or so, you will be able to recall it more or less instantly. If not, one further visualisation, in which you correct a letter you may have got wrong, will be all that is required to remember that word after a further break and thereafter whenever you wish. In fact, you will be able to spell the word 'pyrrhuloxia' for the rest of your life, both forward and backward!

Successful strategies work all the time for anyone who cares to use them. And in the case of spelling, the harder or longer the word, the more useful the strategy. Commonly misspelt English words are not usually as long or difficult-looking as the one you have just mastered, so they can be quickly and permanently memorised using the technique. As we tend to make the same spelling mistakes over and over again (using strategies that don't work) changing from being a poor speller to an excellent speller is not a major undertaking. Typically, it will take closer to a weekend than a year. Bear in mind that as you become skilled at using the new strategy you will be able to use it more efficiently, and quickly. If you are sceptical, find the most difficult word you can in a dictionary and commit it to memory, testing yourself whenever you later call into question your memory or spelling ability. Support your new skill by future pacing what it would feel like to be a master speller. This will change your self-image as a speller which might otherwise reverse your early successes.

Other master strategies

Other strategies have been identified for other major areas such as memory generally, and creativity. People who achieve remarkable feats of memory invariably incorporate visual imagery into their strategy, just like top spellers. There have been plenty of books written about improving your memory, so I will not attempt to add to those here. But suffice to say that many of the basic strategies can be applied generally and bring immediate improvement, without eliciting the detailed strategy of an individual.

Another recurring factor in modelling mastery is an ability to use all representation systems in a highly developed way, and to switch from one to the other. In this way, and this applies especially to feats of memory, combining modalities (being able to see, hear and feel an experience) etches a memory strongly on the brain. Musical mastery, for example, will clearly require an auditory skill. But some aspects of the skill require a strong visual ability, and certainly without feeling there is a limit to the level of skill that will be reached. Real memories are of course multi-modal; you don't recall something as though you were blind or deaf, restricted to one or two senses. So, whatever your thinking preference, it will pay you to use and develop all the main thinking modalities so that you can implement successful strategies of all kinds copied from others.

In other cases mastery strategies are more individual. Two 'masters' might use apparently different patterns, partly based on their preference. So you can choose your favourite model. The important thing is to get better by learning better ways to do things, rather than to find a single all-purpose strategy.

I was fascinated to learn the strategy of a young man who claimed the only thing he was really good at was getting out of bed every day feeling on top of the world and ready for anything. Veteran positive thinkers listened carefully to the step-by-step elicitation of his strategy. It transpired that the first thing he became aware of was sounds, either of birds or traffic. He did not move from his bed at this point, nor did he open his eyes. He then visualised the events of the day that would come up, but concentrated on one activity or event that gave him a lot of pleasure — I recall he was a keen cyclist and swimmer and really enjoyed these activities. He mentally experienced this one pleasurable activity or event, until he reached a pitch at which he *had* to get out of bed because he was so looking forward to what he was going to do — even though it was later in the day! Up to this point he had still not opened his eyes. At the peak of his visualistion he could wait no longer, and shot out of bed, to start yet another day ready for anything and feeling great.

An envious lady questioner asked what he would do if nothing on his day's schedule created a level of ecstasy to ensure his happy state of mind. His answer was naive and pragmatic, but textbook NLP. It never happened; he always planned to do something sufficiently motivating every day, or decided on something before he got out of bed. So early morning blues, it seems, are not genetic, just a matter of the wrong strategy. Strategies for getting to sleep, or being productive in the hour after lunch are just as effective and transferrable.

Coding mastery strategies

Having established a framework based on the three main senses (seeing, hearing and feeling), NLP is able to express any strategy in an easily understandable form which can be used universally. Apart from the main representation systems themselves, we have to know whether the sense is external (sensing 'real' things) or internal (inner representations of these senses). So V^e denotes visual external, which would apply, for example, to a part of your strategy that involved watching somebody, say, doing a sport or showing you how to knit. V^i, or visual internal, denotes an inner visual image, in the way you saw the words in your mind when you were learning to spell. A^e denotes auditory external and A^i auditory internal, which, for inner dialogue, or self-talk, is denoted by A^{id}. K^e is kinesthetic external, and would include the feel of the book in your hand or a headache, and K^i if you imagined stroking a cat or flying.

As I said earlier, what makes strategies unique is their syntax, or the order in which the various representations occur. Our young happy cyclist's strategy for 'getting out of bed feeling on top of the world' went something like: A^e, V^i, K^i: auditory external, the birds or traffic noise; visual internal, seeing the forthcoming day's events, but with eyes closed; and kinesthetic internal, feeling the pleasurable experience, including the water as he swam, or the wind in his face as he cycled. He might well have had an A^i in the middle, as I recall he saw and read off a list of the things he was going to do during the day, and he probably needed all three modalities to create such a strong motivation. Top spellers tend to be V^e, V^i, K^i — looking at the word they want to spell, seeing it internally, then 'feeling' whether it is right.

Try to identify and code some of your own strategies. You might want to include motivation — how have you been strongly motivated? Was it hearing a moving speech, or being encouraged by what somebody said? Some people find music extremely stimulating. Or was it something you saw, or read, a film perhaps? What came next? What happened inside? Is there some feeling you associate with being highly motivated, or some image of the goal you are motivated towards? Try to spot recurring patterns as you explore your strategies. You might want to identify your strategy for fear, loneliness, frustration or other states you might be familiar with — these are things you are able to do well, states you can adopt without really trying. But spend some time on your mastery state because, even without using an external model, this will be your key to mastery in the areas you want to improve.

Identifying detailed mastery strategies

There are universally identified mastery strategies for specific skills such as spelling. But a lot more can be learned about these successful strategies at a lower, submodality level. Having learned what makes good spellers (always), how can we elicit the strategy of master spellers? Knowing that visualisation is the most effective representation system, what submodalities, or detailed strategies, produce true master spellers? We discover this by doing what the founders of NLP started by doing — finding excellence wherever we can and modelling it, both externally and internally. All sorts of activities like spelling, rifle shooting, or preparing dinner for eight, are amenable to eliciting detailed strategies.

In the case of the 'happy riser', for example, we would need to know the submodalities and syntax (order) of each part of his strategy.

- What happened immediately after hearing the sounds outside?

- Was he aware of other sounds?

- Were there any internal sounds, or inner dialogue?

- What was the next internal experience?

- Did the process start with some sort of agenda — a diary page or a written list?

- Were there sounds, or spoken words, or just images?

- Did the images of the day's events come in chronological order, or order of pleasure or pain, or importance?

- What were the specific submodalities of each visualised event (large, small, associated, dissociated, clear, blurred, colourful or black and white)?

- In particular, how did the motivating image differ from the other visualised images?

- Could he, for example, make an event (like going for a simple bicycle ride, or meeting a friend that evening) motivating by the way he created his imagery?

- What were the kinesthetic submodalities, external or internal?

- Did any other external sounds occur during the process, or was he not aware of them after the initial waking up?

- How long did this strategy take each morning?

Simple questions like these can elicit the most complex and masterful strategies. The more detail we get, the easier it is to model the strategy, and the greater chance there is of transferring any state or skill.

Skill in handling numbers fits into a similar category as spelling, because it also requires visual imagery to enhance memory skills. But this is also subject to widely varying and fascinating individual mastery strategies. One seminar delegate, who is very adept at mental arithmetic, described to me 'how he did it'. He saw all the numbers he handled as if in small neon lights, up and to his left. Every number had a different colour: bright, familiar ones for the numbers which were 'easy' to manipulate; and drab, sickly colours for 'difficult' numbers, like prime numbers. Although his description became increasingly bizarre, it represented a consistent, completely dependable strategy which he insisted was 'very easy' to operate and he could 'teach to anyone'.

Mastery modelling is one of the most potent contributions that NLP is making in the whole arena of human excellence. And there is no field of activity that cannot benefit from these techniques.

ANCHORING

Anchoring is another NLP technique which can be applied in conjunction with the mastery exercises you have just learned, to make an even greater impact on your behaviour.

As you know, states of mind can change quickly, usually because of some external stimulus. For example, the sound of a bell can trigger an emotion, a feeling, associated with the end of a lesson at school, your turn in the doctor's queue, or a fire. The sound of a doorbell might bring happiness or fear, depending on who you are expecting. In NLP a stimulus which triggers a physiological state is called an *anchor*. Now that you are familiar with representation systems, you can imagine for yourself lots of anchors involving all five senses. A smell can evoke a memory from childhood; a photograph will do the same thing, as will a tune, or a tone of voice.

Anchors are so common and widespread that we do not notice their existence or, more importantly, how they constantly affect us — changing our state of mind, our whole physiology, from one moment to the next. Advertisers use anchors — brand names, catchy tunes, images or symbols, all the time. As with all the characteristics of our thinking, anchors are useful for survival — red signals mean stop, the smell of smoke means fire. But many of the anchors we respond to unconsciously have long since lost their usefulness. By learning how to create new anchors, we can make this automatic thinking device work *for* us.

Creating anchors

Let us first think of some easy anchors, or triggers, to help us achieve a desired state. Although anchors can be based on any of the five senses, the three main senses — seeing, hearing and feeling — are the easiest ones to use for this purpose. For instance, the visual image of a red light is likely to trigger the stop association of a traffic light. Auditory anchors are everywhere, in particular in the sound, or imagined sound, of words. When you say to yourself 'Steady, now,' it will have a steadying effect, triggering in you a state of caution or steadiness. You don't actually need to hear the words, any more than you have to see a physical red light. It can be an internal sense. If you have ever crossed your fingers in an expression of expectancy, you are using a kinesthetic, or feeling, form of anchor. If you watch athletes or other sportspeople going through their little rituals just before an event, you will see the rich variety of anchors that people use.

Because we shall be using anchors whenever we feel the need to bring about a required state of mind, the anchor needs to be *discreet* — in other words, not obvious to others. (Although beating your breast gorilla-style might induce a dominant state of mind, it might be somewhat career-limiting if observed by colleagues!) Your anchors also need to be *unique* in their purpose.

That is, they should not be the sort of actions you tend to use frequently throughout the day. So, for example, a 'thumbs up' sign, or making a circle with thumb and index finger, whilst ideal in triggering a positive state, would not be unique to the specific mastery state you wish to recall.

So think of three triggers, one using each of the three main modalities. The visual one will be any image that will help you associate with the desired state of mind — perhaps an object from your mastery visualisation. The auditory anchor might be a word, perhaps the word best fitting the state you desire — like confidence, or calmness. The kinesthetic anchor can be an actual touch trigger, such as putting your thumb to the second, or third finger — both discreet and unique. But it might just as well be crunching up the toes of your left foot, or scratching the nape of your neck.

To put these anchors into effect, go back and enter your chosen mastery experience, building up to a climax where all modalities are strong and you experience the overall feeling of mastery. Just as you are entering this state, apply all three anchors, either together or in quick succession. Say the word or words, see the image, and make whatever movement you have decided on. These three anchors are now linked to this experience of mastery. If you are not sure that you have truly relived the experience, or you did not time the anchors at the strongest point, have another go. Further visualisation, using the anchors, will reinforce the association between the anchors and the state of mind.

Future pacing

Now let us put the technique to use. Do a mental run-through of a future occasion when you will want to call on your mastery state. Mentally rehearsing a future event is known as *future pacing*, a term we have already met. Visualise the activity you want to improve, but this time notice what triggers the feelings of inadequacy, fear, self-awareness, or whatever it is that causes disempowerment. It might be stepping onto a stage, entering your boss's office, hearing a particular person's voice, standing up to give a presentation — whatever it is that, usually just prior to the activity, knocks you back emotionally. Having identified this trigger (which is, in fact, an existing, well-used negative anchor), you should run through your visualisation again, and apply all three mastery anchors to instantly recall the state of mind you desire.

Try this a few times. The change in your emotions will probably be instant, as an immediate association is made with your earlier, strong mental imagery, and all the feelings it evoked. If you are doing the exercise with a friend, they will be able to see a change in your body state, your physiology, reflecting the new state of mind. You might like to experiment with applying the anchors in a different order, or together rather than in succession. You might then find that a single anchor (possibly the kinesthetic one) is all that is needed to switch your mental state instantly.

The final stage, of course, is to put this into practice. So allow yourself the opportunity to apply your anchors. The moment you sense the negative trigger, apply the mastery anchors, and enjoy the state of mind you have chosen. Excel in whatever you are doing, and see the difference it makes.

Because of the speed at which it can work, anchoring is a very powerful personal skill. And because you are dealing with long-standing patterns of behaviour, its impact can be disturbing unless you use the technique in a sensible, measured way, gradually improving your subjective skills as you experience incremental, objective — real life — success. Anchors are especially useful when you need to call on particular resources without any warning. In these situations, all you need to be aware of is the negative trigger that tells you you may have a problem. Having already mentally rehearsed your mastery state, and chosen your positive anchors, you then simply use the anchors at will.

Resource anchoring

So-called *resource anchoring* refers to anchors that are associated with different emotional resources, such as confidence, calmness, creativity, assertiveness, etc. To use these, you recall and 'replay' different occasions when you had these states of mind, applying different anchors to each resource. You can then call on a particular resource as it is needed, by applying the different anchors.

NLP has other techniques involving the use of anchors. Some of these are used in treating serious phobias and are better left until you are familiar with the basic skills and have experienced several successes. Other techniques are more appropriate for therapy situations, rather than for DIY use. But you now have a range of skills to bring about fundamental changes, giving you more control over your life, more choices, and a far higher chance of getting what you want.

10

Getting What You Want From Others

▼

ONE OF THE NLP PRESUPPOSITIONS we met in the first chapter was: 'The nature of communication is the response it produces.' However we communicate — in words, in writing, or with body language — it is for a *purpose*. We want to achieve an outcome — perhaps to inform, to warn, to impress, or to entertain. If we achieve that purpose the communication has succeeded, however unconventional or apparently inappropriate the means of communication used. If we do not, it has failed. Product advertisers and company public relations departments are very aware of this rule. They want to see outputs in return for communication inputs. Whether or not a written communication is couched in clear, unambiguous language, or we feel we have got our verbal message across unequivocally, the real test remains the outcome of the communication.

CREATING A RAPPORT

Being able to communicate effectively means being able to achieve your outcomes, your purpose, as affecting, or through others. And this is largely to do with what NLP terms *rapport*. Where there is understanding and mutual respect, even minimal communication will be effective. A glance across a crowded room can convey a clear message between two people where there is already rapport. Conversely, where there is no rapport, a carefully worded statement about 'lay-offs' from the managing director, complete with practised gesticulations and expensive audiovisual support, can convey the wrong message to the assembled employees.

Rapport is not separate from communication. A cycle is at work. You can say something that will create rapport, and the rapport gained will in turn make it more likely that what you say will be understood. But what you say can also cause negative feelings, or break rapport, so it is not enough just to be aware of the words, how they are said, and the accompanying body language. Rather, the total communication can only be measured against its outcome — does it work?

We have already met one important ingredient in rapport — a common preference for a representation system. Two 'visualisers', for example, are likely to get along better than a visualiser and a kinesthetic person in conversation. Likewise, two people with an auditory preference, probably naturally good listeners, and with similar timing and clarity of speech, will get along fine. But you can also create rapport by being aware of a preference, and 'mirroring' the physiological characteristics of the other person, even if your own preferred representation system is different.

Mirroring

Mirroring is something we all do most of the time. If you watch two people locked in conversation you will often notice that their silhouettes mirror each other. They might both be leaning forward, or leaning back with their hands clasped behind their heads, or with their elbows on the desk. They are unlikely to be aware of this mirroring of their body posture, as it is an unconscious, natural way to express rapport. The mirroring might also include speech, pitch and tone of voice, breathing rate, and other physiological characteristics.

Interestingly, two people enjoying rapport might not necessarily share the same interests, or be in agreement about the interests they do share. Rapport is more likely to be due to a common way of sensing and thinking, rather than the content of thought or the subject of communication. But mirroring is also a skill that can be learned, and certainly one that expert communicators are known to practise. By mirroring the body language of the person you are communicating with, in an unaffected way, you can create the sense of rapport that would apply if you were naturally of the same thinking preference. Good negotiators and successful salespeople often exhibit these skills.

But the mirroring technique can be taken a lot further. Body language, we know, can either help or hinder communication. A person sitting back with their arms tightly folded and legs crossed is not, typically, in a very receptive state. He or she is not ready to buy, and the body language is saying 'no' whereas a person leaning forward, looking attentive and animated is probably in a receptive, positive frame of mind. Simply mirroring negative body language is therefore unlikely to influence someone or conclude a sale. However, there is always an unconscious tendency to mirror another person, so it is possible to deliberately bring about changes in a person's physiology, and thus their state of mind, by adopting a speed and tone of voice and 'positive' body language for them to unconsciously follow.

Pacing and leading

Imagine trying to placate someone who is very irate, and is speaking in a loud, high-pitched voice. To achieve rapport you will probably start by matching their voice speed and pitch, to 'become like them', and thus show empathy. Slow, quiet tones are unlikely to 'get through'. The person will not usually relate to a very different mode and tone of communication straight away when they are feeling so upset. However, if you gradually reduce the speed and pitch of your voice they will unknowingly respond, beginning to slow down and become more normal — in fact, more like you. As you slow down your voice and movements further, they will follow your body language and soon take on more rational behaviour, which in turn will make them *think* more rationally. You will have achieved your intended purpose of getting them into a state where they can understand common sense — or, more specifically, what you are trying to communicate. This might sound like magic, but it really does work.

If you are not already familiar with this technique, give it a try. Choose a situation where you need to change a person's emotional state, or make them receptive to what you are saying. The skill lies in not appearing to contrive the situation, and in waiting until the other person has mirrored a small change before moving on to the next one. This technique is known as *pacing and leading*. Many people who we look upon as 'natural' communicators' do this unconsciously all the time. You can use it to great effect in any kind of interpersonal situation.

USING NLP TECHNIQUES AT WORK

The most powerful communication requires a combination of skills. We identify thinking preference by the words and phrases people use (such as 'I see what you mean' or 'I hear what you say'), a range of physiological characteristics, and 'eye access cues'. So mirroring can be combined with the use of appropriate words and body language and observation of other people's eye movements.

Selling

What can NLP offer the salesperson? Having established the thinking preference of a potential customer, what do you do or say to influence them? You can begin by incorporating into your language the words and phrases that fit your customer's thinking style. If you are selling insurance to a kinesthetic person your language might take the form: 'Imagine how you would *feel* if . . .;' 'I'm sure you will *grasp* the importance . . .;' 'Let me *touch* on something else . . '. Although this might sound unnatural, and you might doubt the impact on the person, the effects can be dramatic. You are now, literally, talking his or her language. It only sounds contrived, or strange, because your own preference is different, and you instinctively use different phrases. Through your deliberate choice of language you are repeatedly pressing the button of their kinesthetic way of experiencing reality. If your conversation proceeds to the holiday they will be able to afford when the endowment profits are realised, again your language will be kinesthetic — that is, it will incorporate feelings, rather than the sights and sounds you might otherwise have used to fire their imagination. Not only does language alien to their thinking style waste valuable time, it can actually have a negative effect. It is foreign to their way of thinking, and will therefore tend to be rejected.

Take your kinesthetic presentation a stage further and let them *feel* the glossy literature rather than just see it and listen to your voice. A friendly hand on the shoulder might clinch the sale, whereas it will make a non-touching person want to get away from you as fast as possible! If you are selling a house, let the kinesthetic buyer wander round at his or her own slow pace, taking in the ambience of the place. Don't interrupt with auditory distractions like words. To help the process along, make sure they feel the smooth finish of the mahogany banister, the thick pile of the carpet included in the price, and the texture of the stone fireplace. But most of all, let them linger with any feelings they get. Establish a customer's thinking preference, and use it to gain rapport and a sale.

Mental rehearsal, or future pacing, is another NLP approach used in selling, but it can be equally effective in any situation where you need to persuade someone to do something. As a salesperson you would run through in your mind a forthcoming sales presentation, and visualise the final outcome you want to achieve. Repeated visualisation will build up success memories which will give the confidence that often makes the difference between actual success and failure. There has been lots of convincing research in this area, with sales results dramatically improving following the use of the techniques.

NLP techniques, as we have seen, also help to correct deep-rooted negative self-beliefs, and enable mastery to be transferred from one situation to another, or from another 'model' (such as the company's top national salesperson). Look back at the belief-changing and reframing techniques described in Chapters 4 and 7, and start applying these to selling and influencing others.

Another approach to selling is more pragmatic and says, in effect, that selling is all to do with overcoming objections. If this is the case, then a creative response to any objection is needed. In effect, this involves 'reframing' the question or issue, in order to find another angle that can bypass the blocking objection. In the sleight of mouth and points of view techniques described in Chapter 7, we saw scores of possible ways to crack a seemingly intractable problem or respond to a difficult objection. If you are a salesperson, you can replace the problem statement with the objection, then apply the various perspectives. Choose the better ones, and start incorporating them into your sales presentation when necessary. The whole Meta Model, of course, which is concerned with how words affect us, enables you to carry out similar reframing. ('I can't afford that much . . .' 'What if you could . . . would you then be interested?' And you proceed to show how he can manage the weekly payments, and what he would save on other expenses.)

Giving presentations

In a work situation, NLP techniques apply to meetings, both chairing and participating persuasively and effectively. They also apply to giving any public presentation or speech, whether to a very small group or a large crowd. Of course, there are some differences in a group situation. For instance, when dealing with large numbers of people, you will not be able to determine individual thinking preference (nor would this be of much use). So you will tend to use a variety of communication that covers all three main modalities, to keep the attention of most of the people most of the time. This is why professional speakers tend to use a mixture of audio and visual modes. But fewer people understand that a rich variety of sensual *language* needs to be used — not just words reflecting the speaker's own thinking preference. At the same time, a simple object passed round to illustrate a point — something that can be felt and handled — will do wonders to keep the attention of kinesthetic thinkers. Familiarity with the Meta Model is an asset in any situation where you have to think on your feet. Most 'difficult questions', like sales objections, fit into standard Meta Model patterns. For instance: 'That has never worked . . .' (never, ever?); 'It's obvious . . .' (obvious to whom?). In the nicest possible way, you can always have the last word. As the number 1 phobia in the United Kingdom, public speaking lends itself to NLP techniques that reframe negative self-belief and allow mental 'practice' before an actual speaking event.

USING NLP TECHNIQUES IN RELATIONSHIPS

What applies in a professional selling situation, company meetings and presentations also applies in any situation where we are persuading others, from getting a refund when you return goods to a shop, to getting your children to put things away after them. Most problems seem to involve people and relationships. Take, for example, a common situation where a person you work with just gets under your skin. Other than by being thrown together in the same workplace, you would not dream of associating with such a person. Unfortunately, the demands of your job mean that you do have to relate to the person on a day-to-day, or weekly basis. What does NLP have to offer?

You might start by applying some of the presuppositions we started with in Chapter 1. Remember that your maps are completely different. You each see things differently. You place different emphasis on the same things. He might consider something important which you consider not worth your attention; conversely, what is a priority to you does not seem to even figure in his thinking. To understand that neither of you is able to grasp reality, but has a limited, filtered view of things, can be a humbling process. Insisting that you have some monopoly over what constitutes reality, or right or wrong, is, as well as being untrue, not very helpful — it is unlikely to help you achieve what you want. Better communication is about understanding other people's maps and thus creating helpful rapport rather than winning arguments.

This overlaps with the communication presupposition that what matters is the *outcome*. If one person is able to change your state and affect your goals — maybe your career — adversely, you are clearly not getting what you want from the communication. You need to do something different, so an understanding of the other person's thinking preference is vital. One executive who had ongoing problems with a boss, fresh from an NLP course, suddenly realised that his boss spoke a different language from him. One or two words she used the morning he got back to work gave him a clue; then, sure enough, he found that everything she said was couched in kinesthetic terms. A few days later, when discussing a big report that had already been the subject of a lot of blood-letting, he avoided his usual visual language. ('Can't you see it my way? It looks fine.') Instead he started to use the words she used all the time: 'I've got a better *grasp* of things, this paragraph *feels* a lot better, how would you *feel* if. . .?' He also slowed his fast talking which was obviously causing her annoyance. What might have been a communication impasse was just a matter of appreciating that not everyone represents things in the same way. So start to apply your understanding of thinking preference to *any* communication, and *any* relationship.

Understanding 'life contents' preference

I have found that the different preferences for doing, having, being, knowing and relating that we covered in Chapter 2 can also be a cause of relationship problems. Some people are not happy unless they can see things being *done*. You may have everything under control, and all the information you need, but somehow it comes across to a colleague that you are not doing anything. This can be most frustrating if you feel that the doing part is not important, or that more information is needed before you commit yourself (*knowing*), or that you first have to *get* more funds, people, plant, or whatever. Sometimes a token doing, some semblance of activity, is all that is required to keep them happy. And this action is likely to pay high dividends in improved relationships.

So if you agree to some change in procedures or systems, *do* something. It may be just a start — maybe physically moving a filing cabinet or producing an interim report — anything that demonstrates some action on your part. It might well be that in responding to your colleague in such a way you are also improving your own managerial skill which might be lacking in the doing area. You can soon work out the preference of a colleague by their words and actions, and what seems to annoy them: 'Why haven't you *done* it yet?' 'Haven't you *got* the new valve yet?' 'Do we still not *know* who supplies these?' 'Did you check it's OK with Charlie?' (*relating*) 'I'll *be* glad when these are despatched.' A difference in preferred sequence of life contents between you and your colleague will also account for otherwise unexplained animosity and ill-feeling. 'Why does she have to wait until she gets all the information before getting on with it? At this rate we will be beaten by the competition.' Your cycle of life contents is more likely to result in relationship problems than cultural, political or social differences. As well as being aware of these aspects of our individual maps of reality, we can start using our knowledge to positively improve relationships and help get our desired outcomes.

Managing personal relationships

Reframing is a universal way to create choices, including choices about how you relate to other people. Are there contexts in which your colleagues' behaviour would be acceptable, or even commendable? Are there some aspects of the relationship that are better than others (for example, 'Mark is pretty obnoxious, but at least you know where you stand with him'). Can you reframe things to put them in a different light: 'I only see him at the weekly meeting so it doesn't deserve more than 5 per cent of my attention.'

Is there something specific that bothers you — maybe his tone of voice, or a mannerism? Why not visualise a past communication and change one or two submodalities? To start with, you can give a man a woman's voice, or vice versa, unless you prefer a Donald Duck tone. Or imagine your colleague is about 10 inches tall, and notice the different effect he now has on you. If you switch all the submodalities for empowering ones borrowed from an encounter with a colleague you respect and relate well to, you can change the whole association. Add an anchor to apply when you sense the trigger that changes your state (perhaps the mannerism or the person's footsteps as they approach your office) and you will immediately be able to take control of how you feel.

This will make all the difference to the relationship. You are now in control, and whatever *substantial* problems there are in the relationship (if there are any), you will be able to see them differently, and far more objectively. Most importantly, you can start to make this relationship work *for* you rather than against you. Try out any changes of submodality by future pacing. Run through an upcoming encounter in your mind until you are happy that it no longer triggers the usual response. A few such mental rehearsals will ensure that your brain is reprogrammed and you can play out your empowered state with confidence at the next opportunity.

Keep in mind what you learned in the Meta Model. People we think are assertive or domineering frequently use Meta Model patterns of language as a matter of course. If you fall into their repeated traps you are bound to feel bad about what they say, and the whole relationship. Begin by recognising the patterns, and treating them according to their worth rather than responding emotionally to every unfounded word or phrase. Having responded mentally to what is said, and this changes your whole state of mind (now you are in control, you understand what is happening), you can proceed to use the responses openly and change the whole basis of your relationship. After a dozen or so courteous Meta Model responses it is likely that, whether or not your colleague or boss *likes* you any more than they did, his or her respect for you will certainly rise. Using the earlier techniques to match thinking preference, and the mirroring and pacing and leading techniques we discussed earlier, will get you *liked* as well as respected. These are powerful ways to change a person's perception, without them being aware of what you are doing.

These principles apply in any relationship. Your main relationships might be domestic and social, rather than business, so you may not have a large number of people to take account of. In any event there are usually only one or two people who have a major influence on our lives, in affecting whether we achieve our goals; then a few others who have a secondary effect. So it can pay to get right the few important relationships that most affect how we feel and what we achieve.

Relating to your partner

Although we usually claim to know our husband, wife or partner well, it soon becomes apparent when we meet conflict that our respective maps can be as different as those of casual business acquaintances. The same individual thinking preferences are at work. Does any of the following sound familiar?

The husband arrives home and declares: 'I love you, darling.'

'No, you don't,' his wife replies.

'What are you talking about?' the puzzled husband asks.

'Talk is cheap. You never bring me flowers any more. You never take me anywhere with you. You never look at me the way you used to.'

'What do you mean, look at you? I'm *telling* you I love you.' Something is badly wrong. She wants to *see* things. What she *hears* does not affect her, however clearly her auditory husband tries to get across his message.

Then consider the opposite thinking preferences. The husband shows his love in a visual way, buying flowers and gifts, taking her out, noticing what she is wearing.

One day she says: 'You don't love me.'

He is upset. 'How can you say that? Look at all I've provided for you (gesturing around the room). What about all the places you've been able to *see* on our trips abroad? Can't you *see* that I love you?'

'But you never *say* you love me — you never *say* it.'

'I love you,' the husband yells out, 'I love you,' at a pitch that might be better used to communicate two streets away.

You can imagine how such a mis-match is likely to

render further attempts at communication futile.

And what about the classic modality mis-match of a kinesthetic man and a visual woman? He gets home and gives her a hug.

'Don't touch me' she yells. 'You're always grabbing me. That's all you ever want to do. Why can't we go out to places and see things like other couples. *Look* at me before you touch me.'

With an understanding of how each partner thinks, of course, the smallest behavioural changes will improve the situation. Usually, however, both partners are unaware of the real cause of their 'communication' problem, which might well surface in a different relationship.

Why might this situation arise in a close relationship in which one would expect each partner to be aware of the other's preference? In a romantic relationship the impact of thinking preference is accentuated, so that a little touch, or a special look, or a tone of voice can trigger disproportionate responses. Indeed, observing such a relationship is an object lesson in the power of mirroring, matching representation systems and other NLP techniques. There is a difference, however, in this sort of relationship.

Initially, when we 'fall in love', all three modalities are usually used in the strong desire to please and communicate, so no preference is apparent. The husband used to look at her in a special way *and* buy her flowers, *and* used to touch her with sensitivity, *and* used to speak in a way that she liked. As the force of romantic love wore thin, both partners reverted to their natural preference — the one that they thought was important, because it was important to *them*. Where there is a mis-match, and no understanding of what is happening, rapport is doomed.

This is not to say that we just use one representation system. On the contrary, we all use all modalities all the time, but we have a preference. So, whilst we would want someone to show us as well as tell us that they love us, there will be one way of expressing that love that instantly unlocks our personal representation combination so that we feel totally loved.

Simple mirroring — the eye contact and visual body gestures, the degree of touching and respect for 'personal space', and the tone and speed of voice — would avoid all these relationship problems. Gentle pacing and leading could then bring about almost any change of state desired, especially if accompanied by words that support the other person's preference.

NLP can elicit successful strategies in all sorts of situations, including a romantic relationship. Here is an example of how you can identify your own strategy. It is better if you work with someone else, as your body language usually provides 'answers' more quickly and accurately than verbal, conscious responses. But you can also do this exercise on your own, particularly as you become skilled at recognising the submodalities of your visualisation.

First, try to remember a specific occasion when you felt completely loved. Go back in time and experience to the feeling you had (if necessary get into alpha state and do this as you have done other recall exercises).

Then answer these questions. In order for you to experience these deep feelings of love, is it *absolutely necessary* for your partner to show you that he/she loves you by:

Visual:

- buying you things?

- taking you out?

- looking at you in a certain way?

(The partner helping should watch for signs of affirmation, such as a slight nodding of the head before any words are said, or a change in facial expression.)

Auditory:

- tell you that he/she loves you in a certain way?

Kinesthetic:

- touch you in a certain way?

If you are working with a partner, you may wish to go through the questions again as you become familiar with the different body language responses, checking which is the most positive. You may also wish to recall different past experiences, which might provide further examples of your strategy, and also confirm what you found in the first experience. Now, based on what you have learned about submodalities, elicit the submodalities in each case — visual, auditory, and kinesthetic. Ask, how, specifically? Show me, tell me, demonstrate for me. Identify which characteristics of the visual, auditory or kinesthetic stimuli are important.

As we saw in Chapter 9, as well as identifying the modalities and submodalities of any state or experience, a strategy also has a syntax, or order. The first stimulus might be an external visual one, followed by an inner auditory representation in the form of something you say to yourself, and this might be followed by an inner feeling or warmth, pleasure, peace or whatever, with its own submodalities. So the syntax of this strategy would be V^e (visual external) followed by A^{id} (auditory, internal dialogue) followed by K^i (kinesthetic internal). Or there may be other parts of the strategy combination. Together they form your successful strategy for a particular state or experience — in this case loving and being loved.

In view of the small number of people who usually affect our lives in a major way, it is quite feasible to get to know their strategies. This can be achieved by careful observation (for example, you will recall how eye movements indicate which inner representaions are being made) whenever you converse or interact with them. Knowing and respecting other people's personal thinking strategies will give you the vital edge in any interpersonal communication or relationship.

Understanding personality differences

There is one more aspect of thinking strategy that will help you in your relationships with others. There are strategies that operate at a higher and more universal level than spelling or remembering names; these are more closely related to what we might describe as different personality characteristics. For example, some people tend to notice similarities, while others notice differences. They might be called matchers and mismatchers. In their buying habits, for example, matchers will tend to conform, while mismatchers will buy what is new or different. This high-level strategy operates in the same way as any thinking pattern; it is just a habitual way of looking at things that has formed strong neural highways in the brain. Although this high-level or macro-strategy is a generalisation, because it is easily recognised, it can become a valuable tool in understanding others, even casual acquaintances, to gain rapport.

So what are the other main strategies we can watch out for? One is the way we take account of the views of others, rather than making judgements based solely on our own internal reasoning. Where people 'sort' by their own criteria rather than what others feel and think, they often do not succeed in a service type organisation, where the emphasis has to be on meeting external rather than internal demands. One company used an interview process in which candidates were placed in front of a group to answer questions. As each candidate took their turn, some were clearly not interested in taking on their role as a member of the audience. They were more interested in themselves, and their performance, than their competitors. In fact, the evaluation for the post was based on what the candidates did while in the audience, rather than at the front, as this showed the extent to which they sorted 'externally' rather than 'internally', and the value they placed on others.

Some jobs that do not require interpersonal relationships might well suit a person with more internal values — especially, for instance, an auditor or quality controller who must not be detracted by subjective influences. But most jobs nowadays demand a strong 'people' focus. You can probably place most of your friends and colleagues in one strategy category or another. A similar strategy distinction is whether we need an external or internal frame of reference to measure ourselves against. Some people are simply happy to have done a good job, and their satisfaction comes from 'inside'. Others need to have all kinds of external recognition — a pat on the back, a certificate or promotion.

Another important strategy difference is whether we tend to be motivated towards pleasure, or away from pain. Every one of us is subject to the basic forces of perceived pleasure and perceived pain, and will always tend to move towards pleasure and away from pain. But in some the tendency is stronger one way than the other. Some people will focus their goals and motivation on avoiding losing their job, saving for a rainy day, reducing fuel bills, or not failing in whatever they do. Others will take a more positive view, trying new things, and getting as much pleasure as possible out of any situation.

Yet another high-level strategy concerns whether we are motivated by possibility or necessity. Some people do what they *should* do, or *must* do, while others do what they think they *can* do. We met this distinction in the Meta Model in the form of modal operators of possibility and modal operators of necessity. These two types of thinking use two different languages. As with any universal human characteristic, there are times when one strategy works better than another in different contexts. A job that requires meticulous adherence to rules and systems will suit a necessity thinker, but a task requiring initiative and creativity will require someone who thinks in terms of what is possible.

People will inevitably be a part of your outcomes, or the important ecology on which your success depends. You now have a choice of techniques to create the rapport that you will need if your goals are to be achieved.

11

Your 21 Day Action Plan

▼

NLP IS VERY PRACTICAL, and more and more personal and business applications are being found all the time. The principles of NLP apply to every aspect of human life, and we can all benefit from its simple techniques. NLP lends itself to DIY learning, so you don't have to depend on teachers or follow formal courses. The learning is in the doing. As a subject, NLP is evolving and expanding to meet people's needs in personal development, communication skills and all-round effectiveness. As you learn and apply the skills yourself, and use them in new ways, you will make your own contribution to this emerging art and science. NLP is primarily concerned with the question: 'Does it work?' And if not, 'Can I do something different to make it work?'

Lots of techniques and practical exercises have been described throughout this book. You may have attempted some or all of these. Or you may have read the text straight through intending to do them later when you have a better grasp of what it is all about. In this final chapter I have brought together a series of easily understood activities that will take you right through the main

NLP techniques in 21 days, by action rather than book revision, although you will need to look back at the text to remind yourself of some of the techniques as and when you need them. It is far from exhaustive, but there is no reason why you cannot bring about a very fundamental improvement in your life and ability to get what you want within this period. Three weeks is not a long time in the context of lifelong habits and self-beliefs.

If you have already done an exercise in the 21 Day Action Plan before, do it again, perhaps using a different situation you want to improve. There is always more skill and knowledge to be gained. For example, if you are doing the Day 1 goal-listing for a second time, compare this with your previous list, to see whether there has been any change while you have been absorbing the rest of the subject. NLP is all about thinking skills, and thinking skills are like physical skills in that you need to keep practising them.

This action plan is extremely flexible. For instance, if you think a particular day's activity is better done on a work day, and it falls at the weekend, just switch a couple of days around. Most people who practise NLP find it fun. You don't need lots of discipline to struggle through a painful programme, just the curiosity of a child, a desire to be better, and the courage to change where you need to. The first and most important step is simply to resolve to do all the actions suggested. However, we are all slaves to existing habits and lifestyle, so you may need to use an anchor to remind you of your 21 day commitment — perhaps a word, the number 21, or a symbol you will immediately associate with your plan, maybe on the bathroom mirror, on your car dashboard or a sticker on the front of your work diary — you know what will work best for you.

Day 1

- List your goals and adjust them by asking the questions in Chapter 2.

- Are they specific?

- Are they under your personal control?

- Have you got what it takes to fulfil them?

- How will you know when you have achieved your goals?

- Are they expressed positively?

- Are they at the right level?

- What and who else might be affected by these goals?

Day 2

- Put your shortlist of goals into order using the life contents cycle exercise on pages 35-8. Categorise your goals into *knowing, doing, getting/having, relating and being,* and use the method described to get them into your own cycle.

- Find time to practise relaxing and thinking back to a pleasant memory.

Day 3

- Using your non-dominant hand, list the words that best describe yourself as explained on page 82.

- Choose one negative self-image, and express this as a clear sentence.

- Now decide on the new belief you would like to replace this with.

- Imagine yourself being the person you want to be, and acting in accordance with your positive belief.

- Make the visualisation of who you want to be as vivid as you can, if necessary drawing on how other role models would behave.

Day 4

Identifying submodalities is a basic technique that can be used in many situations.

- First get into a relaxed alpha state as explained on page 67. For this exercise you will need plenty of uninterrupted time.

- Choose two clear memories of past events: one pleasurable memory, where you excelled or exhibited mastery in what you accomplished; and one painful memory, where you did badly, and were perhaps annoyed, angry or embarrassed.

- Go through each modality, seeing, hearing and feeling, and identify as many submodalities as you can, using the checklist on pages 66/7.

Day 5

- Try some more submodality exercises, this time using different experiences — you can cover work situations as well as social and personal.

- Practise recognising as many submodalities as possible, noticing which are common to the positive, pleasurable experiences, and which to the painful, negative experiences.

- While you are doing this, notice whether one modality is easier to recall than the others (e.g. pictures rather than sounds), or whether one of the three main modalities gives you special difficulty.

- Make a note of everything you can remember at the end of each session as you will need to refer to this later.

Day 6

- As you come towards the end of the first week, do a submodality switch between your pleasurable and painful memories by putting the empowering submodalities in place of the disempowering ones. Don't change the content of the visualisation, just the submodality characteristics.

- The more times you do this vividly, the more brain 'recordings' are being made, and the more likely it is that they will be 'lived out' in reality.

- Finally, recall the negative memory with all the

positive thought characteristics, and notice how you feel.

Day 7

- Today, try a submodality switch using the self-image visualisation you chose from your list on Day 3 — how you would like to see yourself.

- Go through the visualisation again, this time incorporating all the positive submodalities you noted on Day 5 when you visualised your positive experiences.

- You can also apply the submodalities of a positive self-image in one area of your life to another area. For instance, if you see yourself as a good organiser, imagine yourself doing things that show this, perhaps some past achievement where you had to use these skills. Then apply the submodalities of this visualisation to the self-image you want to have in another area.

- Do something different today! Change your route to work, move some furniture around, change a long-established habit.

Day 8

- Practise getting into a relaxed, alpha state. Use the countdown method and practise associating with the numbers 3, 2 and 1 as described on page 67.

- Watch out for different high-level strategies in the people you come into contact with. For example, do they tend to move towards pleasure, or away from pain? Do they have an internal or external frame of reference? Check these common strategies by referring back to Chapter 10. Then think of ways you can create rapport with people, based on your understanding of their strategy.

Day 9

- Have a change today. Find some letters, reports or other material you have written yourself, and identify any words and phrases that might suggest a thinking preference — seeing, hearing or feeling.

- Do the same exercise for a few pages of a novel or something else you have been reading recently, and see if you can detect any thinking preference in the writer.

- Chapter 3 will remind you of some common examples of such words and phrases to help you become aware of how our thinking mode is expressed in what we say.

- Do a 50 to 1 countdown. It's a great way to reduce stress.

Day 10

- Stay with language today, but just *listen* — at work, or wherever you are in contact with people.

- See if you can spot expressions, words and figures of speech that suggest a thinking mode, and make a mental note of these.

- From now on you will notice these expressions more; indeed you will probably wonder how you missed them in the past. You are becoming skilled at recognising thinking style, and you can use this knowledge to gain better rapport with others.

- Find time at home to do a 100 to 1 countdown, and just enjoy being down at number 1 for as long as your circumstances allow.

- Deepen your number 2 state by thinking of some peaceful scene that brings you calmness and pleasure — maybe an actual holiday memory, or a secure place you recall from childhood. This can be your Special Place.

- Settle on your 'best' such image and begin to associate this with your 'special' number 2.

- You are now learning to induce your alpha state whenever you wish.

Day 11

- More listening today, but also careful watching. Try to see the relationship between verbal language and body language.

- Notice how fast or slowly a person talks, whether they are 'touchers' or remain distant, whether they need time to think about things or have the answer before you have completed the question.

- This needs enormous powers of observation, which is a valuable skill in its own right, particularly if you are matching the many variables of body language with spoken words.

- Do a shortened countdown from 50 to 1.

- You don't need a lot of time for this, but make sure that the time you allocate will not be interrupted, so you can give it all your attention.

- It is easy to fall asleep during these relaxation exercises, so set your alarm clock if you have things to do afterwards.

Day 12

- Today you will be watching eyes! Notice all the eye movements as you talk to people or are with others as they talk.

- Watch out for recurring patterns, as when people are asked to remember something from the past or to imagine something in the future ('But what if?').

- As you become comfortable with watching, and the high speed at which some people's eyes move, try to relate eye movements to modalities. So, following a question like, 'When did you last see John?' watch out for a visual memory (up and to the left) eye movement.

- Remind yourself of the relevant eye movements if you need to by looking at the illustration on page 58. Otherwise just make a note of what you see in relation to which modality seems to be being used.

- Think of one or two specific things you would like to do or accomplish.

- Do a 50 to 1 countdown.

- As you repeat and visualise the number 2 three times, enter your Special Place.

- When you are mentally and physically relaxed, 'see' your special number 1, visualise your goals as having happened, and enjoy the activities and feelings associated with your success.

- Come back to the objective world by counting from 1 to 5.

- Stop at number 3 and remind yourself that at the count of 5 you will be 'fully awake and feeling fine — better than before.'

Day 13

- Spend today listening for Meta Model words and phrases.

- You will probably need to refresh your memory

by going back to Chapter 8 and reminding yourself of as many of the patterns as possible. Today is just a start, as you are unlikely to remember all the patterns.

- Begin with the ones you find easy to remember. Perhaps the universal quantifiers ('never', 'ever', 'all' etc), modal operators of possibility ('cannot' and 'impossible') and modal operators of necessity ('should', 'should not', 'must' and 'must not') will be enough for the time being. You might also spot complex equivalents, like 'He is not smiling . . . he is not enjoying himself,' where one statement is taken to be equivalent to another.

- Don't worry about the NLP terms, but do try to recognise the different language patterns.

- For the moment, do not respond out loud to these words and statements (however irrational or absurd they now appear to be), although you can begin to think of responses in your own mind.

- Some time today try an even shorter countdown, from 10 to 1.

- If this does not work, go back to 50 to 1, or 100 to 1.

- Before long, you will quickly associate the last few numbers with a relaxed, subjective state of mind, and you can dispense with the preliminaries.

- Incorporate into your Special Place two large screens.

- On one screen you view an existing situation or problem (give it a blue frame).

- On another, to the left as you look towards them, you view the solution to that problem or situation — the picture of the goal accomplished, or belief changed. Give this a white frame. Now you will always associate the different-coloured frames with a problem and its solution, a negative situation and a positive situation.

- Try out the screens with some of your goals — blue frame as things are now, white frame as you want them to be, switching repeatedly from blue to white so you can quickly envisage a change from one scene to the other.

Day 14

- Have some more practice today at spotting Meta Model patterns, but try and extend your range of patterns beyond the list in Chapter 8. Watch out, for instance, for occasions when people are purporting to read your mind.

- As you become familiar with patterns repeating themselves, note how this new awareness affects you. Can you see things more objectively and less emotively? Do you feel more in control of yourself and the situations you are in?

- Now start giving responses out loud, gently and discreetly, using the standard patterns suggested.

- Again, notice how this affects your relationships with others.

- Today, use the skills you have already developed to make some changes.

- Using the top three self-beliefs that you want to change, go through the submodality switching you did on Days 6 and 7.

- Fit this into a countdown exercise, after entering and savouring your Special Place.

- Don't use the screens this time. Just visualise the desired outcomes and incorporate all the positive personal submodalities you have been able to identify so far.

- Make these experiences *real*, as if you are actually becoming a different person. Experience what it feels like to do the things you are visualising.

- Do one more thing. Make a note of possible future opportunities to put into practice the new behaviours or activities that you have chosen to visualise.

- If you already have such situations coming up, make sure you focus your future pacing on these specific opportunities.

- If you have to create opportunities to use your new skills, start arranging them today.

Day 15

- Think of the top three problems or issues that bother you, and express these in simple, written statements.

- Then, using the Sleight of Mouth technique explained on pages 144-7, apply the 13 different approaches as responses to each problem-statement.

- Pretend that they are someone else's problems, and you are responding as a consultant or wise adviser.

- Note down any new angle or idea as it comes to you.

- It is even better if you can get a friend or partner to help you, perhaps taking turns to address each other's problems, as you may get more creative responses.

- You will need to make time to do this at home or during a work break.

- Throughout the day, whenever you hear a negative statement, practise responding mentally, using the Sleight of Mouth pattern. As with the Meta Model, you will probably not be able to remember all 13 perspectives, so concentrate on a few that you find it easy to remember and relate to.

- Try to start making time *every day* to do a relaxation countdown and explore some subjective thoughts.

- This will have to become a habit if it is to give you long-term benefits such as reducing stress and getting things into perspective. In bed, before you go to sleep, is a good time.

- If you find that you always fall asleep you might do your visualising when you wake up in the morning after you have been to the bathroom.

- You only need 15 or 20 minutes, so it is worth adjusting your alarm clock to build this into your daily routine.

Day 16

- The main exercise to practise today is the Points of View technique covered on pages 143/4.

- This is a shorter exercise, so you can apply any number of personal issues you wish, to see whether new light can be thrown on them.

- Don't go for clever-sounding ready-made solutions; just let the 'points of view' work in their own way.

- Sometimes an answer comes in a flash later in the day, or even some days afterwards. It's always important not to try too hard.

- In today's countdown use your visualisation skills to change a well-established habit you want to be free of.

- This time incorporate the anchoring method explained on page 193. You may need to read that section again to remind yourself of the technique.

- If you do this exercise in the morning, watch out for triggers during the day that let you know when you need to apply your anchors.

- If you do the exercise at night, put it into practice the next day.

Day 17

- Do some more anchoring today, but this time choose one or more empowering *resources* (like confidence, calmness, assertiveness or creativity), rather than a specific habit you want to change.

- Apply different anchors to each resource, as explained on page 197.

- Use your countdown time to do the necessary visualisation.

- Whenever you become aware of the warning trigger, apply the anchor you set for the habit you wanted to change in yesterday's activity.

Day 18

- Be on the lookout for false friends — 'Try harder,' 'Be perfect,' 'Try to please someone,' 'Hurry up,' 'Be strong' See if any are used.

- Concentrate your visualisation time on becoming a master at something you are currently only reasonably efficient at. This can be a sport, craft or other skill, or an activity you have to do from time to time in your work.

- Remind yourself of how you can tap into your mastery state by looking back at Chapter 9.

- Commit yourself to an opportunity to put your mastery into practice.

- Change some routine today. Do something

completely out of character, and note how it affects your view of things and people.

Day 19

- You will have fun today doing some mirroring, as described on page 200.

- Avoid obvious facial tics and other embarrassing mannerisms but, as far as possible, copy body language, and see what effect this has on rapport.

- Watch other people in conversation and see for yourself how mirroring is used all the time.

- As you gain confidence in discreet mirroring, you can begin to try pacing and leading. It is good if you can build this into some specific, regular, interpersonal job you have — like selling, negotiating or disciplining, to see the difference that mirroring and pacing and leading makes.

- Link today's visualisation with these exercises, future pacing the interpersonal situations (including the mirroring, pacing and leading) and successful outcomes.

- Think of some new activities you can get involved with that will enhance and support your desired goals and self-images.

- This might involve joining a local club, subscribing to a magazine, taking up a new sport or hobby, reading a book a week, learning a language — or whatever.

- Decide on some empowering activities and do something to commit yourself today.

Day 20

- Be alert today, more aware of what is going on than you have ever been.

- Use all your five senses: listen to words; watch body language; try to feel what others are feeling; listen for new sounds that you have not noticed before; see things you have not been aware of before.

- In your countdown exercise today, see how far back you can go and still recall vivid memories.

- See what details you can sense from times in the past when you experienced mastery.

- Watch out for submodalities you have never noticed before.

Day 21

- Get into your alpha state.

- Then use the old affirmation: 'Every day, in every way, I'm getting better and better.'

- Repeat it as you come out of alpha using your 1 to 5 count-up.

- Think of some other dynamic beliefs (check on dynamic and static beliefs on page 97) and use them as affirmations throughout the day.

- Sometime today, when you are feeling under pressure, do a quick 5 to 1 countdown, to experience immediate relaxation and get yourself into a resourceful alpha state.

- Use this whenever you need to. It will add years to your life, as well as giving you a better state of mind every day.

- Go somewhere on your own with your thoughts and a notebook and write down what you have learned in the last few weeks — the changes in your thinking or behaviour, and any differences in your priorities.

- What, today, are your main goals in life?

- What do you believe about yourself that you did not believe three weeks ago?

- Finally, write down your own action list for the future.

- Decide where you want to be, and what you want to do over the coming weeks, months and years.

- Write down the goals you will have to achieve and the actions you will need to carry out.

- This is *your* plan for mastery and success — you are the architect and builder of your own life. You must decide what you want. Then the new art and science of NLP will help you to get it.

Further Reading

Alder, Dr Harry, *The Right Brain Manager* (Piatkus Books 1993)

Bandler, Richard and Grindler, John, *Frogs into Princes* (Real People Press 1979)

Lewis, Dr David, *The Alpha Plan* (Methuen London Ltd 1986)

O'Connor, Joseph and Seymour, John, *Introducing Neuro-Linguistic Programming* (HarperCollins 1990). Includes an extensive reading list.

Robbins, Anthony, *Unlimited Power* (Simon & Schuster 1986)

238

INDEX

Piatkus Business Books

Piatkus Business Books have been created for people who need expert knowledge readily available in a clear and easy-to-follow format. All the books are written by specialists in their field. They will help you improve your skills quickly and effortlessly in the workplace and on a personal level.
Titles include:

General Management and Business Skills
Beware the Naked Man Who Offers You His Shirt Harvey Mackay
Be Your Own PR Expert: the complete guide to publicity and public relations Bill Penn
Complete Time Management System, The Christian H Godefroy and John Clark
Confident Decision Making J Edward Russo and Paul J H Schoemaker
Energy Factor, The: how to motivate your workforce Art McNeil
How to Implement Corporate Change John Spencer and Adrian Pruss
Influential Manager, The: how to develop a powerful management style Lee Bryce
Managing Your Team John Spencer and Adrian Pruss
Outstanding Negotiator, The Christian H Godefroy and Luis Robert
Seven Cultures of Capitalism, The: value systems for creating wealth in Britain, the United States, Germany, France, Japan, Sweden and the Netherlands Charles Hampden-Turner and Fons Trompenaars
Strategy of Meetings, The George David Kieffer

Personnel and People Skills
Dealing with Difficult People Roberta Cava
Problem Employees: how to improve their behaviour and their performance Peter Wylie and Mardy Grothe
Psychological Testing for Managers Dr Stephanie Jones

Presentation and Communication

Better Business Writing Maryann V Piotrowski

Complete Book of Business Etiquette, The Lynne Brennan and David Block

Confident Conversation Dr Lillian Glass

Personal Power Philippa Davies

Powerspeak: the complete guide to public speaking and presentation Dorothy Leeds

Presenting Yourself: a personal image guide for men Mary Spillane

Presenting Yourself: a personal image guide for women Mary Spillane

Say What You Mean and Get What You Want George R. Walther

Careers and Training

How to Find the Perfect Job Tom Jackson

Marketing Yourself: how to sell yourself and get the jobs you've always wanted Dorothy Leeds

Perfect CV, The Tom Jackson

Secrets of Successful Interviews Dorothy Leeds

Sharkproof: get the job you want, keep the job you love in today's tough job market Harvey Mackay

10-Day MBA, The Steven Silbiger

Ten Steps To The Top Marie Jennings

Which Way Now? - how to plan and develop a successful career Bridget Wright

For a free brochure with further information on our complete range of business titles, please write to:

Piatkus Books
Freepost 7 (WD 4505)
London W1E 4EZ

PIATKUS

Dr Harry Alder is a businessman working with major companies to help their staff reach their maximum potential. He is a colleague of John Seymour, author of *Introducing NLP,* and a leading practitioner of NLP in the UK. Harry Alder is the author of *The Right Brain Manager* (Piatkus), and co-author of *NLP in 21 Days* (Piatkus).